D1568770

# The Official Guide to Coin Collecting

by

## Brad Mills

ISBN   87637-238-8

Library of Congress Catalog Number 73-93248

PRINTED IN U.S.A.

# ACKNOWLEDGEMENTS

The Author, Editors, and Publishers wish to express our thanks and appreciation to these individuals and organizations.

*To Mike Brownlee, Dallas, Texas, for his generous assistance in furnishing a large number of photographs.*

*To Maurice M. Gould, Sepulveda, California, for his encouragement and use of certain illustrations.*

*To John N. Rowe III, Thomas C. Bain and Jack Whitehurst, Dallas, Texas, for advice on the technical aspects of this manuscript.*

*To Clifford Mishler, Numismatic News Weekly, Iola, Wisconsin, for specialized photographs of unusual interest.*

*To Margo Russell, Editor, Coin World, Sidney, Ohio, for illustrations relating to specialized numismatics.*

*To Edward C. Rochette, Editor, The Numismatist, Colorado Springs, for assistance with specialized illustrations.*

*To Q. David Bowers, Hathaway and Bowers Galleries, Inc., Santa Fe Springs, California, for valuable suggestions.*

## ABOUT BRAD MILLS

Author of 1,000 articles on numismatics • An active coin collector and researcher since 1927 • Guest speaker on the Linkletter House Party TV and radio show • Acted as a special consultant to fans writing about coins • Columnist for DALLAS MORNING NEWS • A 35-year member of American Numismatic Association • Past President of Dallas Coin Club • Member, Texas Numismatic Association • Charter Member, Dallas Press Club • Life Member of Sigma Delta Chi, professional journalistic fraternity • Appointed by President as member of the 1967 Assay Commission • An active speaker before coin clubs and associations.

# Contents

# Some Preliminary Thoughts on Collecting

The discovery that certain coins are scarce (1) usually follows an honest and thorough survey of current supply and demand, (2) projected needs of the future for coins of low mintage, and (3) the fact that certain potentially strong series have not been exploited to any marked degree. Trends in coin collecting are exactly like styles in clothes or entertainment habits of the public. Eventually every series will have its day, and along with the upsurge in popularity certain shortages of low dates and mint marks of the particular series will emerge. Frequently acute shortages will appear in a very brief time. Therefore, the favorite game among collectors is to find and acquire potentially scarce coins before their paucity is known by almost everybody.

Thus the entire scheme of the hobby represents a vast change from the old collecting school of 40 years ago, when profit and business acumen were secondary to the sheer joy of ownership. The present rush to smoke out scarce coins that have been largely overlooked is a gradual build-up that was occasioned by the large profits made by the more analytical collectors who suspected the dormant rarities would come to life in due time. And they did, as several million collectors rushed into the hobby for both pleasure and investment. The entire numismatic hobby has undergone a radical change, as evidenced by a review of activities since 1963. Where collectors of 1940 merely desired to own and display rarities, they now have moved into the conglomerate ranks by buying, selling and keeping coins as the occasion demands. From a rather casual hobby, numismatics has become a "search and acquire" project that keeps looking to the future. Collectors who keep studying mint reports in their race to find "sleepers" should not be criticized for their efforts, since many, by actual experience, have been forced to pay more than twice the former value of coins when such coins actually were needed at slightly later dates. This has particularly applied to key coins that were not acquired through neglect or mere procrastination. Thousands of times collectors have suspected certain coins were potentially scarce, but gambled there would be no immediate advance. It usually is best to acquire rare or key coins as they are needed for basic purposes.

# CHAPTER ONE

# Basic Elements of Coin Collecting

*U.S. Peace Type Dollar,*
*1922 Obverse*

The most profitable of all hobbies during the past 25 years undoubtedly has been coin collecting, known professionally as the field of numismatics. In the United States alone there are at least five million serious collectors, and perhaps another five million persons who are searching and culling coins with the hope of finding rarities that are thought to be in circulation.

The great modern upsurge in numismatics started about 1948 and since that time the demand for scarce coins has been unprecedented. Of course, a few minor slumps have occurred but the basic demand for the worthwhile items has been constantly in evidence. Obviously the millions of novices who entered into the frenzied activity learned the hard way that coin collecting requires a good basic knowledge of the hobby.

There were not enough scarce coins to supply the demand after 1950, and soon collectors, hoarders, speculators and accumulators were grasping and bidding high for items that formerly were regarded as commonplace. Selective buying went out the window, as the plunger remarked to himself, "How long has this been going on?"

The ten-fold increase in the number of collectors so swelled the market potential prior to 1965 that speculative and almost hysterical influences naturally entered also. However, the old conservative fundamentalist has existed all along, and a friendly battle has raged continuously between the "quality" collectors of really rare coins and the admitted accumulator who insists he is buying rather common coins on a type of "investment" basis that will be in tune with future spirals.

Many business men with lots of money and little knowledge of the hobby have entered the field on advice of friends, dealers and coin "brokers", and during certain spurts bought so heavily that shortages were created in many common issues that would not have sold at all 20 years ago. This action stirred up the small-time collectors who joined in many exciting trends and ventures. Where acquisition was based largely on rumor and speculation, purchases of common coins did not always prove profitable.

However, all of this is required to make a leading hobby, and every collector must learn from his own mistakes. Possibly some of the speculative practices of today may appear rather conservative tomorrow. The puritanical approach may be the choice of the veteran numismatist who buys only rare coins, but the modern wheeler-dealer of this period feels in the mood to buy, sell, hoard and dabble in all types of issues.

Coin collecting is a very contagious and infectious habit. A young and cautious collector will buy a scarce coin for $10, then upgrade his tastes until he may pay $100 or even $1,000 for a really rare item with a pedigree. Some single coins have been sold for as much as $100,000, while a $10,000 transaction is not spectacular.

The field of numismatics is so wide and varied that most collectors specialize in certain phases. To acquire one each of all United States coins that have been minted would require several million dollars. Out of sheer necessity most collectors must buy what they can afford. Ancient, foreign and United States coins are the principal classifications, each of which may be broken down into copper, nickel, silver and gold varieties. Paper money and medals are generally included in the group.

The dream of finding rare coins in circulation intrigues most new collectors and they laboriously look through current denominations of coins now available in rolls with the hope of discovering a 1909-

*From the Indian Head Penny to the Silver Dollar*

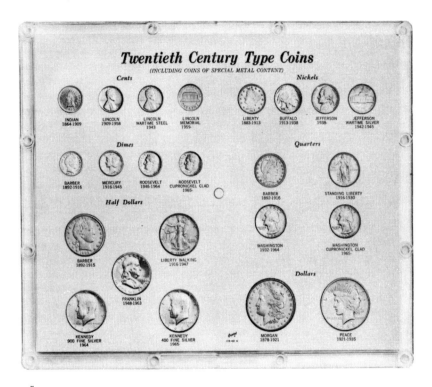

*A Complete Set of Coins Designed, Minted and Circulated in the United States. This Type of Set is Now Very Popular

*Does not include clad, silverless half dollar and clad, silverless Eisenhower dollar*

SVDB Lincoln cent, a 1950-D Jefferson nickel or certain late coins needed to fill spots in coin boards. Countless millions of coin holders have been sold to novices who immediately appear on their way to fortune.

Since 1955 perhaps two million collectors have regularly been taking home great quantities of ordinary coins from banks in a giant effort to find scarce and rare dates that do still exist undetected. This tremendous "stripping" action has so depleted the scarce coin supply still in circulation that the habit has become a very discouraging one. Yet scarce and even rare coins are occasionally found by the most persistent searchers. What to hold out and keep can be both an irritant and problem, since the catalog value of many common coins is misleading unless properly equated.

Naturally the thought of finding a valuable coin in circulation appeals to every fledgling, but eventually the serious collector faces up to reality and starts buying scarce and rare coins from dealers and other collectors. Face value means little and he feels proud of himself when he spends $100 for a Lincoln cent he tried to find for nothing. Once the ice is broken, he usually spends whatever he can for what he wants.

So great has been the upsurge in coin collecting that it undoubtedly has become the nation's largest hobby in volume of sales and general interest.

Any collector today, young or old, should carefully "think out" a buying plan for the future. History certainly will repeat itself if proper thought is exercised in purchases. The average numismatist starts his hobby with a disorganized mind and certainly no true objective, but he usually learns quickly through serious application.

It is much better to mix purchases of scarce and even rare coins with the commoner ones, than to pursue a course that ultimately will give an inventory of bulk and no quality. There can be no greater thrill than "breaking over" occasionally and acquiring a really choice coin. If purchased at a reasonable price, the odds are highly in favor of the buyer of quality. But substantial enhancement should not be expected the next month. The demand for really scarce coins has been gradually upward for more than 20 years. However, it may not be wise to pay exhorbitant prices for rare coins simply because they are needed badly for the moment. More will be said later about the new or plunging collector who will pay almost any price to acquire coins to display vanity and perhaps status. Some semblance of balance must be maintained in both buying and selling.

Many of the older collectors "lucked out" after 1938 simply by putting away four or five rolls of every mint issue as they were available at face value each year. If this had been done since 1920, any seasoned collector of that period would now be much more than a millionaire! It is difficult to believe that a roll of 40 uncirculated 1927-S quarters with a face value of only $10 will now bring upward of $25,000. Of course, we cannot dream of such lost opportunities, but doubtless many fine values are available now for collectors who are able to smoke out coins with a genuine potential.

Frequently coins with high mintage (large numbers coined) are for the moment in very short supply, and collectors must have them to complete dates, types, etc. Extreme caution should be exercised in purchasing such coins at excessive prices, and particularly so where there is a good possibility they may show up later by the roll or sack.

Starting in 1962 millions of scarce and rather rare silver dollars were released at face value without warning by the United States Mint. Prices dropped from as much as $1,000 each to a few dollars each, and near-chaos was the result. The Mint had been hoarding these dollars from 60 to 80 years, then almost suddenly decided to release them. They were readily available for a time in $1,000 bags at face value. Included were the formerly scarce dollars from the Philadelphia, New Orleans and San Francisco mints.

Another mint release of this kind will never occur again, but the giant distribution of scarce silver dollars in the early 1960s emphasized the necessity for care in acquiring temporarily scarce coins that may be released in quantity from some later source.

Even the silver dollar deluge gave the hobby great momentum and publicity. So thrilled were collectors to get a recently rare dollar for less than two dollars, they bought them by the thousands as a speculation. And what a wise investment those purchases turned out to be! All silver dollars now command substantial premiums, and more will be said about this big hunk of metal later. Dollar collectors are numbered by the hundreds of thousands, and up to now it looks as if they could do nothing wrong.

It seems that some collectors simply can't find themselves in the right boat when certain coins stage sensational advances or gain in popularity. Yet it looks relatively easy for other collectors to participate in most of the upward surges. The real reason is that the wise, selective collector reasons out his portfolio, while the careless accumulator believes everything he hears and buys without a definite objective. Diversification is very important, both from a pleasure and profit standpoint.

It never is well to go off the deep end when coins are changed to a new design or type, such as cents, nickels and dimes. Almost invariably a new type coin is hoarded for months, following wild rumors that the design was wrong and will be called in soon. This

| Coin Roll Or Set | Face Value | 1974 Value | Enhancement |
|---|---|---|---|
| 1948-S Cent | $ .50 | $ 19.00 | $ 18.50 |
| 1949-S Cent | .50 | 30.00 | 29.50 |
| 1955-S Cent | .50 | 12.00 | 11.50 |
| 1948-S Nickel | 2.00 | 33.00 | 31.00 |
| 1949-S Nickel | 2.00 | 44.00 | 42.00 |
| 1950-P Nickel | 2.00 | 45.00 | 43.00 |
| 1950-D Nickel | 2.00 | 340.00 | 338.00 |
| 1951-S Nickel | 2.00 | 100.00 | 98.00 |
| 1952-D Nickel | 2.00 | 50.00 | 48.00 |
| 1955-P Nickel | 2.00 | 30.00 | 28.00 |
| 1949-P Dime | 5.00 | 400.00 | 395.00 |
| 1949-S Dime | 5.00 | 600.00 | 595.00 |
| 1950-S Dime | 5.00 | 360.00 | 355.00 |
| 1951-S Dime | 5.00 | 275.00 | 270.00 |
| 1955-P Dime | 5.00 | 37.00 | 32.00 |
| 1955-D Dime | 5.00 | 20.00 | 15.00 |
| 1949-P Quarter | 10.00 | 400.00 | 390.00 |
| 1951-S Quarter | 10.00 | 260.00 | 250.00 |
| 1955-D Quarter | 10.00 | 85.00 | 75.00 |

*(Continued on next page)*

happened with the 1883 Liberty nickel, the 1913 Buffalo nickel and the 1938 Jefferson nickel. The 1883 Liberty or "V" nickel was so heavily hoarded that it is today the cheapest of all Liberty nickels, yet it is the oldest. A very mild exception to this rule is the 1964 Kennedy half dollar, a coin that has consistently commanded a small premium since its original issue. This coin will be discussed later in more detail.

The future holds a tremendous potential for the collector who gives proper study to the hobby. Naturally a good numismatic library will add much to the knowledge of the novice. It is impossible to collect coins intelligently without at least a few basic books to authenticate them. It is better to know what you are doing than to live in a kind of fool's paradise. In spite of all of this, millions of happy collectors go merrily along their way, and it may be said that

| Coin Roll Or Set | Face Value | 1974 Value | Enhancement |
|---|---|---|---|
| 1948-P Half Dollar | $10.00 | $150.00 | $140.00 |
| 1949-P Half Dollar | 10.00 | 500.00 | 490.00 |
| 1949-S Half Dollar | 10.00 | 430.00 | 420.00 |
| 1950-P Half Dollar | 10.00 | 285.00 | 275.00 |
| 1953-P Half Dollar | 10.00 | 220.00 | 210.00 |
| 1955-P Half Dollar | 10.00 | 120.00 | 110.00 |
| 1950 Proof Set | *2.10 | 120.00 | 117.90 |
| 1951 Proof Set | *2.10 | 80.00 | 77.90 |
| 1952 Proof Set | *2.10 | 50.00 | 47.90 |
| 1953 Proof Set | *2.10 | 33.00 | 30.90 |
| 1954 Proof Set | *2.10 | 18.00 | 15.90 |
| 1955 Proof Set | *2.10 | 21.00 | 18.90 |
| 1958 Proof Set | *2.10 | 9.50 | 7.40 |
| 1964 Proof Set | *2.10 | 4.75 | 2.65 |
| 1968-S Proof Set | *5.00 | 5.00 | .00 |
| 1969-S Proof Set | *5.00 | 5.00 | .00 |
| 1970-S Proof Set | *5.00 | 9.00 | 4.00 |
| 1971-S Proof Set | *5.00 | 5.50 | .50 |
| 1972-S Proof Set | *5.00 | 5.50 | .50 |
| 1973-S Proof Set | *7.00 | 14.00 | 7.00 |
| TOTALS | $184.30 | $5,225.25 | $5,040.95 |

*Issuing Price

most of them have lucked out on coins purchased after 1950. The housewife who scans every coin in her purse soon learns she must know more about the coins she is looking for.

Collectors who put aside uncirculated rolls of ordinary U. S. coins during the past 20 years have profited handsomely from the easy effort. The same condition applies to proof sets that were available since 1949 at regular issuing prices. The following tabulation graphically shows the surge in a few of the rolls or proof sets that could have been acquired at time of issue by any collector with a bit of patience.

Certainly not all uncirculated coin rolls held out each year will do as well as those listed above, but other phases of coin collecting will fill the void if the collector will give proper thought to the dozens of scarce coins and rolls that have not yet come into their own. Both the conservative and speculative groups will derive fun and profit from the hobby if they will learn more about it. Great opportunities exist for all who join the parade and keep both feet on the ground.

Value of a coin depends chiefly on (1) rarity, (2) condition, (3) popularity, and perhaps (4) age. Other factors may be involved but age alone seldom takes precedence over rarity. A full chapter will be devoted to rare coins versus the more common ones, a rather controversial subject between the conservative collector and the speculator who buys coins in quantity with the hope of acquiring "sleepers" that eventually will be in great demand.

Type coins represent the simplest and perhaps the most sensible way to cover the complete range of numismatics. Even so, the collector with modest means will not find it easy to acquire all the types he knows he should have to approach completeness. A type coin is one representing any date of an identical series, such as a Roosevelt dime, a Liberty "V" nickel or a Morgan type silver dollar. Obviously the objective of the type collector is to acquire one coin of as many types as possible, as opposed to the all-out collector who wants every date of every type. The type collector's motto is, "To have one is to have all."

The "set" collector is one who wants every date and mint mark of any one series, such as Roosevelt dimes or Franklin half dollars. He also is the one who keeps looking through his change for the dates and mint marks of Lincoln cents and perhaps Washington quarters he does not have. Most of the coin collectors now active started in this manner, and especially those with limited means.

Key coins are the scarce ones found in almost every series. They include such items as the 1950-D Jefferson nickel, 1932-D Washington quarter, 1909-S VDB and 1914-D Lincoln cents, 1916-D Mercury dime, etc., etc. They are extremely hard to find in circulation.

Sound advice to any new collector would be:

1. Buy the best you can afford.
2. Expand coin education with good books and catalogs.
3. Take good care of all coins.
4. Buy scarce key coins with confidence.
5. Acquire early and historical coins that are basic to numismatics.
6. Check carefully before cleaning coins. They may be ruined.
7. Upgrade your collection as you can with choice specimens.
8. Assemble nice type sets as far as possible.
9. Learn to identify counterfeit coins.
10. Buy coins for pleasure, investment or speculation if you can afford it.
11. Establish yourself with good coin dealers.
12. Grade fairly.
13. Deal honestly.

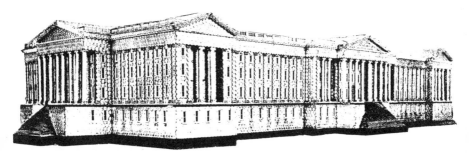

*The U.S. Treasury Building Reproduced in Souvenir Half Dollars*

# Rare Coins
## Versus Common Groups

# CHAPTER TWO

*The Controversial 1804
Silver Dollar*

Select any 10 coin collectors at random and you will find that each person had a different reason for starting the hobby. One became interested when a few old coins were given to him; one was intrigued by some obsolete coins he had never seen; another read a juicy advertisement on how to make a fortune on coins; a nervous old bachelor felt it would help occupy his time; a thrifty housewife started scanning every piece of money passing through her hands; a speculator sensed the investment opportunities offered; a wealthy man decided he would make a showpiece of his collection, and perhaps a novice entered via the hoarding route when he heard silver prices were about to rise.

Scramble them all together and you have a composite of Mr. Coin Collector. And what a rugged individual he is! The silver coin, the scarce coin and the rare coin are in immediate danger from the gobbling up process exhibited by such a vast drove of avid collectors. A common coin badly needed by a young collector to fill a place in his holder is as important to him as the $1,000 coin is to the veteran numismatist.

It has been said that every coin collector pursues the hobby exactly as he lives in general. The conservative person is extremely slow to venture out into the expensive brackets, while the big spender wants the best the market affords — and right now. The net result is a fairly balanced demand for all types of numismatic material. Occasionally a collector with strong frugal instincts remains so miserly that he cannot rise above the face-value complex. He is the casual accumulator who keeps looking through his pocket change with the hope of finding something really rare. But even this person may eventually graduate to a collector who finds pleasure in the more expensive items. Perhaps we should not be too hard on the collector who tries for a while to find a bird's nest on the ground. He may one day buy our entire collection at a good price!

A full tabulation of coins ranging from the most common to the rarest would require several pages, but a few of the major groups should be listed as a rough guide for the collector who may wish to follow at least a general plan. Immediately involved are both United States and foreign coins in all metals and states of condition. The new collector should quickly develop an objective of some sort, and where he is trying for enhancement he should make a close study of past performances of the issues involved. Even if the collection is being formed chiefly for enjoyment, it is wise to pursue a sound purchasing policy applicable to both inexpensive and rare issues.

Broadly speaking there are six groups now being held in collections, as follows:

1. Face value coins only, such as those still obtainable in circulation, or in uncirculated condition at a bank. Even some coins in your pocket could be included in this group. Such issues are considered fringe or marginal material.

2. Low premium coins that probably have been thrown aside, kept in coin holders or found in circulation over the years. These are the issues just now beginning to command premiums because of age, a slight scarcity or promotional activity. The Kennedy half dollar and various silver coins issued between 1955 and 1964 would be included in this group. Nearly all uncirculated nickels, dimes and quarters minted prior to 1964 command small premiums, even by the roll. Hundreds of foreign coins struck since 1900 also would be included in this broad classification. The very old U.S. coins in badly worn condition are generally considered low-premium items unless of the rare dates and mints.

3. Medium premium coins that have a ready market value at some figure above face value, such as the better circulated issues with

some age, or the fairly recent uncirculated coins more than 15 years old. All of these coins would be considered scarce enough to be classed as numismatic items among average collectors.

4. Key premium coins in all series, usually valued from $10 to $50. Such items are those that must be purchased at coin stores or from other collectors. Occasionally one may be found in circulation by the ardent searcher who refuses to give up.

5. Key premium coins of the better grades, and any of hundreds of rare coins valued from $75 to $500. The scarcest dates of Indian Head cents, Barber quarters, silver dollars, etc., would be good examples from this important group. Various gold coins and foreign rarities also would be included. Surprisingly enough, many of these coins are dated after 1900, with scarcity and not age being the controlling price factor.

6. The very rare coins of all types, denominations and ages that are valued from $500 to more than $10,000. Prior to 1950 only a few coins were valued at more than $2,000. Now they are listed by the dozens where top condition prevails.

Each of the foregoing groups could be broken down further to include all of the coins in any collection, but only a general classification could be shown as a rough guide to values in a very swift-moving hobby. The smaller denomination coins usually carry much higher premiums, percentagewise, than the higher denomination silver and gold pieces. This would be particularly true with the rare one-cent pieces.

The following mixed tabulation will show the remarkable enhancement in various rare coins during the past 20 years, as based on average selling prices:

| Coin | Condition | 1949 Price | 1974 Price |
|------|-----------|-----------|-----------|
| 1794 Silver Dollar . . . . . | Very Fine | $650.00 | $7,500.00 |
| 1799 Silver Dollar . . . . . | Uncirculated | 75.00 | 3,500.00 |
| 1804 Silver Dollar TII . . | Uncirculated | 3,125.00 | 125,000.00 |
| 1889CC Silver Dollar . . | Uncirculated | 10.00 | 1,600.00 |
| 1893S Silver Dollar . . . . | Uncirculated | 130.00 | 14,000.00 |
| 1903O Silver Dollar . . . . | Uncirculated | 200.00 | **40.00 |
| 1928P Silver Dollar . . . . | Uncirculated | 4.00 | 115.00 |

*(Continued on next page)*

| | | | |
|---|---|---:|---:|
| 1794 Half Dollar . . . . . . | Fine | 50.00 | 550.00 |
| 1878S Half Dollar . . . . . | Uncirculated | 300.00 | 8,000.00 |
| 1949P Half Dollar . . . . . | uncirculated | .50 | 25.00 |
| 1936D Quarter . . . . . . | Uncirculated | 9.00 | 240.00 |
| 1916D Dime . . . . . . . . . | Uncirculated | 100.00 | 700.00 |
| 1921D Dime . . . . . . . . . | Uncirculated | 11.00 | 500.00 |
| 1885P Nickel . . . . . . . . | Uncirculated | 25.00 | 300.00 |
| 1926S Nickel . . . . . . . . | Uncirculated | 60.00 | 350.00 |
| 1939D Nickel . . . . . . . . | Uncirculated | 2.00 | 35.00 |
| 1877 I.H. Cent . . . . . . . | Uncirculated | 45.00 | 700.00 |
| 1909S I.H. Cent . . . . . . . | Uncirculated | 28.00 | 200.00 |
| 1909SVDB Cent . . . . . . | Uncirculated | 17.00 | 170.00 |
| 1914D Cent . . . . . . . . . | Uncirculated | 17.00 | 500.00 |
| 1923S Cent . . . . . . . . . | Uncirculated | 12.00 | 200.00 |
| 1860D Gold Dollar . . . . | Uncirculated | 300.00 | 6,000.00 |
| 1795 Gold Eagle . . . . . . | Uncirculated | 200.00 | 4,500.00 |
| 1856O Double Eagle . . . | Uncirculated | 250.00 | 10,000.00 |
| 1880 Gold Stella . . . . . . | Proof | 1,000.00 | 35,000.00 |
| *Estimated | **Effect of Dollar Dumping by U.S. Mint | | |

It would be foolish to drool and dream over what we missed, except that the foregoing table tells an important story we cannot ignore. The coins listed may or may not show a rapid future enhancement, but other issues will. The pleasure collector may insist he merely acquires coins for the fun of it, but he usually is the first one to tell you about the tremendous profit he has in his holdings. And who can blame him!

For the collector who thinks the rare coins are too rich for his blood, there are just as many opportunities in the lower brackets.

Selectivity and diversification will place the smaller collector in as strong a position as the wealthy collector enjoys, while his percentage of enhancement may be even better. A table similar to the one above could be shown by using the low-price coins that have acted equally as well since 1949. The face-value coins put aside as uncirculated rolls in the 1940s are now a great comfort to the collectors who were thoughtful enough to do it. Hoarding on a grand scale is not recommended, but it is always smart to cover the field.

What then can a collector do to continue sensibly on his way to certain numismatic objectives? The situation from an economic standpoint is not radically different from investing in stocks and bonds. The safest way in either is to acquire and hold basic items of proven quality and performance. Where pleasure is the chief pursuit in the hobby, buy all across the board with the best possible balance between rarity and the more common issues. Such a course usually means money well invested along a route that began as a casual and relaxing venture. Few hobbies have such a high profit potential.

The field of numismatics has assumed such giant proportions that the average collector frequently becomes lost in the razzle-dazzle of developments and trends. It is no wonder that the novice finds it difficult to separate the single scare or rare coin from the common bulk material he can buy at the same price. Actually both courses may prove productive where selection has been narrowed to the live items.

Coin shows and large conventions are held by the hundreds each year, and in any area it is possible to drive to at least one show or local bourse over a weekend. The minute the collector hits the door he makes for his favorite dealer with a want list, or perhaps he has a bunch of material to sell at top dollar. If it were possible to follow the first 10 collectors entering the bourse, we could easily see why there are so many tastes among the hobbyists. Of the small number of collectors under surveillance, two or three would be looking for the common material, three or four for the medium scarce coins, rolls, commemoratives, etc., and three or four for the rarer and more specialized items. About half of the 10 would have profit in mind, while the other half would be seriously considering coins with genuine numismatic value.

Countless thousands of casual collectors remark, "Oh, I am just piddling around," when asked about their activities. The word "balance" immediately comes into the picture when a coin portfolio is considered today. It is neither safe nor wise to condemn any phase of buying that has been highly successful in the past. Personally we may abhor many of the past practices that seem in conflict with the more basic hobby, but eventually they may prevail against what appear to be reasonable trends. The heavy speculative influences of the past were possible because of the demand from millions of new collectors who were willing to buy the common coins that formerly had been ignored. The dabbling tendencies toward recent coin rolls, circulated coins that formerly had no premium value, and in fact all types of inexpensive material came about largely because there was an acute shortage of rare material among millions of new collectors.

Where is the line of demarcation between a common coin and a rare coin? Now wouldn't somebody ask that question! To say that such a division between the two is a matter of taste would be to brush off the question as something relative. Actually we have the "scarce" group between the common and the rare, but attempts already have been made to define the principal groups in a broad way. This subject is brought up again simply because many collectors claim some of their coins are rare when they are only scarce.

A Lincoln cent costing no more than 10 cents is common; one selling for a dollar is scarce; another listing at $10 is very scarce; one offered at $50 is medium rare, while one selling for more than $250 is very rare. All of the ordinary Indian Head cents are in the low scarce bracket and are very nearly in the common group. Any attempt to list all degrees of scarcity for *all* coins would require several pages.

When a collector insists on acquiring only the common and medium-scarce coins, he should confine himself as much as possible to the uncirculated items. Where this is not possible, he should make sure that his circulated coins (singles or rolls) are of the so-called "staple" or standard items that have maintained value and respect over their short history. Many of the circulated coins minted after 1940 are highly marginal and are in poor demand on the market. They are useful in filling blank holes on coin holders, for trading purposes and for possible enhancement, but they are not sure sellers. There is a wide range of quality within the common groups. Even the face-value hoarder and accumulator should avoid late issues with a high mintage, except for a roll or two.

The question of interest rates on money invested in coins is a big factor and will be discussed at more length in a later chapter. To the collector of the common issues it is important to realize that money invested in most places earns around five percent. Unless, of course, he is a purist and dabbling around strictly for fun! Whether you are a collector of common or scarce coins, have at least one good reason for making a purchase. If it is purely for fun, more power to the hobbyist.

The roll situation will keep bobbing up as we go along. A scarce or even medium rare coin may be held in rolls by veteran collectors who acquired them when the coin was very cheap and considered common. A close check usually will show that the lucky roll owner put the coins away many years ago because of the short mintage that year, and not necessarily on a random basis. Conversely thousands of inexpensive rolls are now held by the younger collectors and speculators who hope to luck out on a few issues in future years.

In general, the common versus rarity premise applies equally to single coins and rolls. However, a few exceptions exist where very few rolls of large issue coins were put away in uncirculated condition because of carelessness or economic conditions. World War II years were a notable example of this void, when the silver nickels were all but ignored through four years of continuous coinage. A few of the smart collectors did save uncirculated rolls of the 11 silver nickels as a kind of "poor boy" set, a neat bit of thoughtfulness that has returned a profit of about $700 on each $22 invested. It looks now as if any alert collector should have been excited over a radically new wartime nickel containing 35 percent silver and nine percent manganese. But roll collecting was in its infancy during those troublesome years.

Less than 20 years ago the collector of common coins stood neck-deep in all kinds of opportunities. The substantial premiums asked in 1973 for the dozens of coins that were readily available around 1950 at face value, or a little more, readily attests to the fact that little thought was given to the splendid chances then afforded at banks or on the open market. Both circulated and uncirculated groups were included.

Perhaps the same collector is today at least knee-deep in the same opportunity, if only he can be selective enough to take the right position on common coins with a real potential. They may be those that already are commanding slight premiums, and not the giant issues of clad coins minted after 1964. With millions of collectors in the vast search for both pleasure and profit, certainly not all will pay strict attention to the many coins that are bound to advance in both interest and price. Extensive hoarding is not recommended, but the neophyte who is groping around for a course to pursue should conduct a little research of his own into the various issues.

Rare coins are found in every U.S. series, with the exception of a few of the most recent issues that were minted only in large quantities. Starting with 1793 and coming all the way up to 1955, the finicky collector has a wide choice of rarities that should satisfy every taste and requirement. Foreign rarities are equally as desirable and date back to the early Grecian period.

This seems to be an excellent time to acquire the rare U.S. coins that are below their former peak selling prices. This would include the best key coins in all series minted after 1860, good examples being found in Indian Head and Lincoln cents, nickels of all types, dimes, quarters up to 1937, half dollars and silver dollars.

The rare key coins now seem to be particularly good where it is still possible to complete date and mint mark sets, and they should continue to increase in value. A few of the hundred such coins are the 1877 and 1909-S Indian Head cents, the 1909-SVDB and 1914-D Lincoln cents, the 1916-D Mercury dime, the 1916 Standing Liberty quarter, the three 1921 half dollars, and the rarest of the Washington quarter series. Obviously a complete set of any issue must include the rare coins along with the common ones, a fact that gives the upper-bracket collector the edge over the novice who may wish some day to break over and pay high prices for the key coins he could have bought at one time for much less.

We know that many of our most famous collectors of today started as mere accumulators, only to realize as they went along that the rare coin, if bought right, seemed to carry the prestige, pride and hope that the common one did not possess. Many of the large collections formed prior to 1950 are now worth from four to 20 times their original cost, with rarities perhaps playing the biggest role in the spectacular enhancement.

Yes, rare coins have been a good investment.

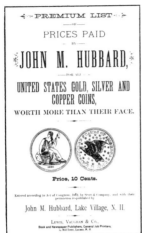

# CHAPTER THREE

# Buying and Selling Coins

*Price List From One
of the "Original" Dealers*

Buying and selling coins involve so many angles that the new collector may become lost in his attempt to pursue the hobby in an intelligent manner. The beginner who first picks coins out of circulation will soon find that face value means little in the advanced field of numismatics, and almost suddenly he enters a new world where there is a heavy exchange of coins at all kinds of prices. Most of all he doesn't want to appear too amateurish, but this fact can lead to a lot of trouble.

It is difficult for a novice to adjust himself to such new and thrilling surroundings without falling into an occasional booby trap. Even the most experienced collector has many times found himself on the wrong side of deals that were completed because he had not kept abreast of the market. Acquiring coins immediately involves (1) a knowledge of condition, (2) genuineness, (3) title if seller is an itinerant, and (4) a study of prevailing prices. All of these factors will be discussed in greater detail in later chapters. No attempt is being made to frighten the young purchaser, but a very comforting feeling accompanies transactions completed at reasonable levels.

The most gullible buyer or seller is the one who refuses to acquire reliable catalogs, periodicals and current information on trends and values. Not much better is the experienced collector who stays mostly by himself, refuses to join a coin club, and lives in a hazy world of numismatic ignorance. This kind of man may be either a plunging type of loner with plenty of money to throw around or an introvert who operates at one of two extremes — penury or flamboyancy. All of these special conditions are mentioned as high spots only, and not as a general warning that the hobby has become a tricky one. Growth has been so fast that the neophytes need some special assistance.

The serious collector soon finds his way around and becomes familiar with both buying and selling methods. Before long he has used one or more of the many services open to him as outlets for an expanded interest. There are a hundred ways to acquire coins but the usual contacts follow as a general guide:

1. Coin stores
2. Bid boards
3. Bourses and shows
4. Other collectors
5. Advertisements in coin periodicals
6. Auction catalogs (consignments)
7. Trips and vacations
8. Banks and payroll contacts

It is interesting to note that the novice buys ten times as many coins as he sells. He loves them to death for a while, then gradually learns to sell the duplicates as if they were horses or cattle. However, a few of the oldtimers claim they never have sold a coin under any condition. That may be carrying matters a bit too far.

Too much emphasis cannot be placed on the importance of a good coin dealer, the one who never dreads to see a customer re-enter his place for fear of a complaint. He is the merchant who constantly strives to keep faith with collectors and knows he must deal fairly to maintain continuous relationship with the public.

The dealer who buys and sells coins on the premise that perhaps he will not see the customer again should be avoided, but he is strictly the exception that may be found in any line of business. Occasionally such a dealer may operate a concession in a tourist area, or in a leased space where vacation and casual traffic is very heavy. This would particularly apply to places like Hong Kong, Singapore,

Cairo, Caracas and World fairs, where antique and coin dealers bid heavily for the tourist trade. This situation will be discussed in a later chapter. Even most of these shops are legitimate in their own way, but some counterfeit coins have been innocently purchased by travelers who were looking for bargains.

A lot of fuss should not be made over the bad features of buying and selling coins. Numismatics has become a giant hobby and a big business, but the fact that as much as a 20 percent range in prices of various items may be found is alone a good reason to dwell on the importance of education through comparison.

In any issue of a current coin journal, prices may vary enough to make the reader wonder how the upper bracket advertiser can move his coins at all. Actually he can't, where the quality is identical. But in the case of circulated rarities, the dealer asking the highest prices may offer the best values because he is grading more realistically than the other dealers with the lower prices. More will be said about the importance of grading in later chapters. Even a half grade may make a big difference in the value of such circulated rarities as the 1877 Indian Head cent, a 1936-D quarter and a thousand other issues.

A wide range of full-time dealers may be found in the various cities of any size. Others advertise extensively and operate only by mail. A city the size of Dallas, Houston or San Francisco may have more than 25 coin stores, while in New York City, Chicago and Los Angeles numismatics has reached giant proportions with almost every type of outlet.

Proof sets and silver dollars — excellent gift items — were the opening wedges where large general stores have installed attractive coin departments as new ventures in merchandising. Gold coins also have caught the interest of that portion of the public that just now is flirting around the fringes of numismatics. About 15 years ago prominent department store chains in more than 20 cities decided to handle coins on a regular charge basis. This practice has dignified the hobby and made it a regular part of the total business, although some of such coin departments still are operated on a leased arrangement. These booths also are a large outlet for coin supplies.

Resort spots sell more coins to visitors than to home folks. In such small localities as Knott's Berry Farm in California, and Hot Springs,

Arkansas, local coin shops are aimed toward visitors who may be surprised at an opportunity to indulge in their favorite hobby while on vacation. Gold coins, proof sets and silver dollars are particularly offered to the visiting public as the more staple and acceptable items.

A recent and effective buying and selling medium is the bid board. This type of merchandising usually is maintained by dealers who staple large numbers of coins on a big board in the form of a public, weekly auction. All items are in plain view and usually graded or described to satisfy the average buyer. In some states such an auction board is legal only when the operator forms a club and sells memberships to prospective buyers and sellers. The seller pays the operator a commission for use of the board, while the buyer pays only the amount of his successful bid, plus the applicable sales tax. Some boards of this type display more than a thousand items each week, with the bidding becoming most intense during the last day of the auction period.

The seller who places too high a limit on such consignments obviously must bid them in with his own membership number, and pay the commission for his bad judgement. However, it may be wise to consign coins on a strictly highest-bid basis, and especially so where they are good movers. Near the end of the auction period the sellers crowd into the large room to check on their consignments, while the buyers do the same thing in an effort to bid successfully at bargain prices on coins of their choice. The last-minute rush may run the prices of many coins to very high levels, due to the determination of competitive collectors to obtain items for their personal collections.

The ease with which the choice coins sell, as opposed to the slower bidding action of the less desirable ones, plainly proves there is no substitute for quality. On the whole, a bid board represents a reasonable buying and selling medium for most coins, but the entire perspective should be appraised before offering for sale those coins that plainly fall outside the normal bidding habits of the membership. The very rare and expensive coins might not move at all on a bid board in a small city, where the same items would bring satisfactory prices in Los Angeles or Houston.

Buying and selling coins at bourses and shows afford an opportunity to deal in plain view across the table. At the recent American Numismatic Association meeting in San Diego more than 125 dealers offered coins worth millions of dollars, and most were as anxious to buy as to sell. At lesser shows and bourses the same opportunities exist. The collector who shuts himself off from meetings of this kind is bound to miss the exposure that goes with real numismatics. Here is where he really learns his way around.

The keen shopping and comparison going on at large bourses is extensive but it frequently pays off. At the beginning the collector rush at the opening bell is terrific. Buyers quickly make the rounds with the hope they can fill their want lists from dealers who have the scarce and rare coins marked realistically. Vendors who suddenly find themselves doing a rush business usually stop and check with competitors to determine whether they have been selling coins below the going prices. All of which proves that even the best dealers have their troubles in keeping up with the market.

The very close-buying collector may all but wear himself out in making the rounds at large conventions where he would like to purchase coins at attractive prices. Being a very frugal buyer, such a person may wait until the last hour to approach the seller with a low offer. But he usually finds the coins were sold just before his last contact.

The safest shopping or selling method applicable to bourses involves a quick check to determine the trends in vogue. Then the buyer or seller should complete his deals while both supply and demand are good. If selling, the collector may not want to sacrifice desirable coins where the market is temporarily depressed. This is particularly true of such coins as commemoratives and items having good past performances. It is not smart to become panicky over market trends affecting issues known to fluctuate.

Buying or selling among collectors represents a direct, interesting and frequently amusing means of disposal or acquisition. The friendly bickering, claims and counter-claims, fussing over condition, reports that Dealer So-and-So would like to have the coins in question at even higher prices, and all of the usual sparring among traders are parts of many bartering sessions.

It is better to consider all angles of a swapfest than to rush blindly into a confirmed deal that sounds too rosy. However, the intelligent collector may hold his own in such dealings if he is well enough informed. Around any coin club the hard trader will be encountered, the one who claims to have the finest material for sale and the highest buying prices for whatever he needs. This type of peddler is the exception, not the rule, although he may appear at meeting after meeting with his little bag of overpriced and overgraded coins.

The experienced hobbyist should enlarge his acquaintance among collectors, even nationally if necessary, to establish an expanded buying, selling and trading base. State sales taxes do not apply to such casual transactions among real hobbyists, a situation that will be explained in another chapter. The most successful collector keeps a notebook with the wants of other collectors prominently displayed. Such contacts generally start at meetings of coin clubs, conventions and the usual outside social activities.

The mature, benevolent numismatist who counsels patiently with the young collectors is the hobbyist who does most to advance coin collecting along a healthy route. He trades back and forth with the youngsters on a fair basis, encourages them to acquire the better material, shows them how to grade coins, and never misuses his superior knowledge. In later years the advanced students can point with pride to the coins they have acquired from their mentor.

Unfortunately an occasional sharp operator will take advantage of the novices who unwittingly fall into his confidence, but in due time they will learn from experience they have been taken in by a cunning collector whose chief aim was to unload coins at exhorbitant prices. Such a shady trader will be found in any hobby, and coin collecting should not be blamed for the few bad apples in the barrel. Coin clubs and associations have done much to eliminate the questionable collector, and more will be said about this phase of numismatics in a later chapter. The beginner will make a few mistakes in his early eagerness, yet he nearly always survives his errors.

Many reputable coin periodicals are available, and all try hard to keep their advertising on a truthful basis. Strict rules require advertisers to meet certain standards that involve (1) grading, (2) genuineness, (3) prompt shipment to purchasers, (4) clear title and (5) return privileges. Since buying coins by mail is something of a "pig-in-a-poke" transaction, the purchaser usually is protected to the extent that he must be happy with the items. Both buyer and seller are protected by state, postal and interstate laws, a fact that places mail transactions on a dignified and safe level.

Occasionally a buying or selling advertisement will appear that should immediately arouse suspicion on the part of the reader. Where a buyer is offering to pay a very high price for all coins delivered to him; or a seller promises to deliver coins at bargain prices, it might be well to check into such offers before sending either coins or money. By using a post office box on a temporary basis and a swindling scheme of some sort, a few dishonest advertisers have over a period of years bilked collectors out of both coins and money before the schemers were apprehended. This practice is so uncommon that the average collector will never encounter it. It is always wise to check on all mail orders that have not been acted on within a reasonable time.

Advertisements in periodicals may be used to advantage by collectors who wish to buy or sell coins on a kind of retail basis. It is not unusual for an advanced or elderly collector to use a full page or more in a grand attempt to dispose of his coins at satisfactory prices.

The buyer who believes certain coins are selling at prices too low, frequently advertises to buy such coins at stated prices. It is often difficult to tell whether the advertiser sincerely wishes to acquire the coins, or to promote them because he already has a large inventory of the items sought. This type of promotional merchandising is legitimate, but it might be well to check carefully on the scarcity of the coins wanted. The advertiser could have a good point. The coins may be scarce.

A good coin periodical is an absolute necessity for any coin collector. The advertising serves as a continuous catalog and a trend medium that may save the subscriber both time and money. The buying and selling prices shown by many dealers are an immediate clue to their respect for various items offered. Every type of collector will at some time use the columns of periodicals for buying or selling coins, or at least they will serve him well in his dealings through other means.

Use of auction catalogs for buying and selling coins is perhaps the oldest of all merchandising methods in numismatics. The practice started almost 100 years ago when some of the first large collectors and dealers wished to dispose of their rarities. Essentially the auction catalog is just what it represents: a means of selling coins, paper money, etc., via the catalog route. The dealer who runs the auction charges the seller or consignor a percentage of the selling price for the service. Items are numbered in the catalog and fully described. The auctioneer may be selling part of his own coins, along with others consigned for the catalog sale. The buyer pays no commission, but postage and insurance are added. Percentage charged for selling coins in this matter varies from 10 to 25 percent.

So-called "mail bid" auctions are carried as advertisements in many coin periodicals. The buyer merely sends his bid to the advertiser and hopes for success as the top bidder. Occasionally a limit is placed on the various items offered in an effort to discourage very low bids that might be successful. The mail bid route may work very well where the seller is trying to dispose of a large number of inexpensive items.

The dedicated coin collector uses part of vacations and casual trips for smoking out rare coins in remote and unsuspected places. In small county seat towns he goes to the post office, county clerk and newspaper office, and asks for the names of local persons who may have old coins. One collector found an unbelievable number of scarce and rare coins in a small Washington town while visiting there. The same collector placed a small advertisement in a rural Colorado paper and was able to buy a large collection of Indian Head cents. Several retired hobbyists spend all of their time in traveling over the United States, with the exclusive hope of finding old coins. As a rule it is difficult to buy coins from a novice who has inherited them, since any show of interest on the part of the purchaser arouses immediate suspicion.

Bank tellers and payroll clerks are excellent contacts for the collector. They can be helpful in finding scarce coins, as well as useful in obtaining certain rolls that may be needed. In 1952 a half dozen tellers in a large bank kept a sharp eye out for 1950-D Jefferson nickels and were able to find more than 500 in a short time. A collector bought them at a small premium and they are now worth about $7 each.

# CHAPTER FOUR

# Knowledge in Numismatics

*1876 Twenty-Cent Piece*

To make a hard, technical course out of coin collecting would scare away most of the hobbyists and take the whole endeavor out of the pastime category. This would never do, but some objective should be set up to justify a desire for additional coins and the time spent with them. The drop-outs usually are those who refuse to increase their knowledge as the decisions become more difficult and expensive.

In any new endeavor the average person tends to believe himself more advanced that he really is. The old saying that "a little knowledge is a dangerous thing" certainly applies to coin collecting, but perhaps in an innocuous way. Where the beginner is having his fun as a strict amateur, "To heck with a few mistakes," probably describes his dream world adequately. Millions of neophytes have boldly stepped into the hobby through a dozen doors, and it may be truthfully said that most of these enthusiasts have oriented themselves toward more enlightened levels.

There are two principal ways to start collecting coins. The most common involves a carefree, enthusiastic and trusting course that usually is precipitated by a desire to find, buy or hoard any inexpensive coins that are available as possible collectors' items. Even with its many faults, this is perhaps the most enjoyable course to pursue and the one most of us have taken. While going through this period we believe most of what we hear, while accumulating a large inventory of face value and low premium coins that the veteran collector generally avoids. Also included in this group are the housewives and the gullible who are constantly looking for the end of the rainbow.

A second way to join the hobby is via the careful, frugal and academic route. This course usually is pursued by the adult who is the studious type, a cautious individual, or the wealthy neophyte who wants to make sure of his ground before advancing into the expensive realm. Such a collector treats the hobby as if it were a grand venture. The older beginner is, on the whole, much less daring and effervescent than the youngster, probably because he mostly starts with the better grade of coins. However, a man can be far too cautious in normal buying pursuits, even in the case of high-priced rarities.

The big plunger will be described in some detail later. He is the all-conquering beginner who pays high prices for everything he can get, frequently as a matter of show. He is the collector who is badly in need of numismatic knowledge and doesn't know it. He also is the opposite extreme to the over-cautious novice who acquires material on a very timid basis because he is in need of additional information on the various issues.

Every coin collector will eventually realize his shortcomings, but this is no guarantee he will do anything about it. Constant study and some expense are required as the novice bowls along into new and advanced channels, yet he may elect to stumble forward on a strictly pleasurable binge. Many of the most casual collectors give no special time and allot no regular amount of money toward acquiring coins.

Knowledge is so broad, so all-present, so general that it actually is a part of every section of this book. Perhaps this chapter should have carried a more direct, educational title of some nature, although knowledge in its broad sense is a specific for any type of coin collecting.

Any beginner who tries to learn about either general or designated phases of the hobby is doing what comes naturally along a course that leads to self-improvement. Many collectors are too lazy and careless to attempt to separate hearsay from facts. Or do they choose

31

to use the hobby as a relief from everyday tension? If so, please forgive the author for prodding them along.

Recently a collector fell heir to a large collection of ancient coins. Previously he had no urge to obtain items of this type, a fact that made him almost helpless in the attribution of his new windfall. Obviously it was necessary to obtain a few good books, catalogs and reference booklets relating to Greek, Egyptian and Roman coins. It is refreshing to note that the lucky recipient became an expert on almost every phase of ancient coinage. He soon became intrigued with the historical background of the various bronze, silver and gold coins that dated back to 400 B.C., and later became almost a pest in his efforts to interest *all* collectors in the very old issues of the Ancients.

In all honesty, the casual collector will do well to specialize in a limited manner that will not make his research appear to be hard work. Many advanced numismatists use most of their spare time in a study that may even be equipped with cameras, but such anexpanded effort is hardly recommended for the ordinary collector. Lecturers and authors prepare their learned papers from the work done in well-equipped studies, while the really wise men are in great demand as expert witnesses in court and estate matters.

Most of all, the collector should not make his hobby a form of drudgery by over-research or studying the most minute angle of every small transaction as if it were the family jewels. This statement may seem to be in contradiction with advice given earlier, but it really isn't. The greatest pleasure and profit come from relaxed buying and selling with the thought that the transaction seems logical. The informed collector simply pursues his hobby with the hope that both fun and profit will be a natural result.

One of the greatest collectors in the country offers the following advice:

1. Join a local coin club if possible
2. Join a numismatic association if old enough
3. Subscribe to at least one good coin periodical
4. Obtain printed information on grading
5. Purchase reference books on various issues or groups
6. Purchase annually at least two good catalogs

7. Attend bourses and conventions
8. Visit public libraries often
9. Visit back and forth with fellow collectors

Each collector can find a reference to fit his individual needs, even if it proves inadequate in spots. It is well to remember that a good sailor always carries a compass. The greatest enjoyment comes from having related information on various phases of the hobby. One small book may suffice for some phases of numismatics, while even three or four reference works are required in others. Good auction catalogs are valuable, since they accurately describe and illustrate items of unusual interest.

Special courses in numismatics have been offered by Massachusetts Institute of Technology, Roosevelt University, Long Beach City College, Southern Methodist University and many European universities. Coins do not start and end with those carried in the pocket. Some are as rich in history as are the famous works of art.

Many of the largest banks have permanent coin displays that will inspire any visitor. The Smithsonian Institution has on display a coin collection that is perhaps unequalled. No type of store window will attract more attention than the one filled with coins, unless it is one filled with beautiful dancing girls.

A few true but rather amusing stories will be related to illustrate the various degrees of gullibility, cautiousness, ignorance and wisdom of a wide cross-section of coin collectors. They will plainly show that time frequently takes care of the meek and the blind. But they also prove that wisdom is still a jewel.

While going through the Denver mint in the summer of 1926, a tourist-collector asked the guide whether the 1926-D nickels being coined that day could be obtained at the mint. The guide told the visitor that they could not furnish the nickels directly, but the bank across the street would be glad to give him an uncirculated roll of 40. He added that the roll would make a good souvenir of his visit to the mint. The tourist became busy and forgot to obtain the roll of nickels. The 1926-D nickel today catalogs at about $300 each, or $12,000 for a roll of 40. The disappointed visitor (your author) has since had a very red face because of his carelessness.

The oddest part of the whole Denver mint episode was that the guide made the casual remark as the group left the premises, "You'd better get a few of the Denver nickels this year. Don't look like we are going to run off as many as usual."

Luck sometimes is on the side of ignorance. Between 1955 and 1960 an old lady living in the Arkansas delta country near Memphis kept telling a neighbor that she had a big batch of old coins. Oh yes, she would sell them, but each time a visiting collector called on the elderly lady, she would stall around and promise to sell them the next time the visitor was in the region. Finally in 1963 the visitor appeared, and the coin owner said she was ready to sell if she could get top dollar. The collector, armed with catalogs, could hardly wait to sift through the group of old coins. His sharp eye fell on a nice silver dollar that had some possibility, and quickly he noticed it was a 1904-0 specimen with very little circulation. Here he could not resist giving the poor old woman a mild lecture. He told her that in 1960 he would gladly have paid $200 for the dollar, but now he would not give her even $3 for it.

Our collector friend tried hard to explain that the Treasury Department had dumped perhaps two million on the market and had driven the price down to an absolute minimum. However, the old woman told the visitor she would not sell him any of the coins under any condition, since he had given himself away with such a thin story. The remainder of the coins consisted of badly worn Indian Head cents, a few "V" nickels and a general residue not worth more than $75.

The incident illustrated two points very well. First, our elderly lady shouldn't have held out so long before showing the coins; and, second, the collector was saved close to $200 because he would have purchased the 1904-0 silver dollar in 1960, although knowing it would have been a very dangerous risk.

The average collector develops a terrific complex on entering a coin store. He sees the display walls lined with specialized books of all kinds on coin collecting, then realizes how inadequate his library really is. Perhaps he should not feel so guilty, since any hobby may be pursued with varying degrees of intensity. More than half of all casual collectors buy a single catalog that seems best to fit their purposes, then joyfully thumb through it with the finality that makes it a kind of bible.

Collectors are geared to the hobby with the flexibility that goes along with any casual undertaking. It is better to shoo them gently into a more knowledgeable course than to crowd them into an embarrassing position requiring regular study periods.

Encouraging students in the pursuit of knowledge is the dullest, most skipped-over chapter in any book. Such narration always takes the form of lecturing, urging and even preaching of a kind hardly acceptable to the average student. In the case of a pure hobby, it may be better to make a game of the improvement effort than to suggest it as a definite chore. How many graduates of high schools and colleges continue advanced work in English and mathematics? Very few, but those who do are seldom looking for jobs.

A good example of thoroughness that should be mentioned is the large book published about 20 years ago on the early American large cents. This volume was laboriously but happily written by Dr. William H. Sheldon in a brilliant effort to identify and describe the hundreds of die varieties of so-called "large" U. S. cents minted from 1793 through 1814. The author was able to find more than 70 varieties of 1794 cents, and his classic description of each variation included enough information to classify with ease any large cent owned by any collector. Even the amateur cataloger can get a big thrill from the positive identification of his large cents while using Dr. Sheldon's book. The volume also contains a new approach to grading and appraisal practices.

The author receives hundreds of letters each year from non-collectors and beginners who think they are in all kinds of trouble. About half of these communications relate to a few old coins found around the house, and nearly all owners feel they have valuable items. The other half are from novices who mostly have a large number of recent coins with little or no premium value. A surprisingly large percentage do not even own a coin catalog. A small sprinkling of letters is from owners or collectors who really have valuable coins and merely want additional information and encouragement.

The beginner who chiefly looks through loose coins or goes through rolls obtained at the bank should know exactly what he is looking for. He should know from memory the dates and mint marks worth keeping. When he doesn't, he will hold a marginal coin in first one hand, then the other before finally making a decision. The chances are he will hold it for a while, then compromise by keeping it. Of course, there is a very fine line between the keepers and some of the more common ones. Many of the coins thrown back into circulation 10 years ago now would command at least nominal premiums, but time alone has been the principal enhancement medium.

While on a buying trip through the Mississippi delta country in the late 1950s, an antique dealer visited in a large plantation home. He was informed by the lady that she also had a gold coin collection for sale — strictly at "catalog" prices. When shown the magnificent gold collection, the dealer could not even produce a coin catalog, although he was in the market for rare coins of any kind. The old Southern belle casually brought out her own catalog and offered the coins at listed value. The antique dealer was afraid of his own judgement and would not pay the full price asked. He begged off, returned to Jackson and found that the coins were worth twice the price asked.

How could this have happened? It was simply because the catalog used by the plantation lady was at least 12 years old, and our antique hero was not well posted on quotations. He rushed back with an offer to buy the coins, but our good lady became suspicious and did some checking on late prices herself. The net result was the sale of the coins to a wealthy collector who was delighted to get the dozen or more rare "C" and "D" mint gold pieces. Thereafter the antique dealer carried his coin catalogs.

It is impossible for every collector to know everything under every condition, but it certainly pays to avoid a compromising situation where a good chance to buy coin collections must be passed up because of a lack of knowledge. Conversely, the daring collector or dealer frequently pays too much for coins when approached by a clever seller who tells of the virtues of an offbeat collection he needs to sell at once.

And it is always wise to beware of the owner who has been offered such-and-such for coins that are very slow movers. They may or may not be an acceptable buy.

Knowledge is a commodity any collector cannot have too much of!

# CHAPTER FIVE

# Counterfeit & Altered Coins

*1883 Nickel, Obverse and Two Reverses*

Counterfeiting in its strict sense is the making of bogus coins and currency. The circulation of such spurious imitations adds to the offense and becomes part of the crime. Irregular practices of this sort have been pursued since around 600 B.C., or soon after the earliest coinage of the Lydians and Greeks. Long regarded as one of the most serious crimes against a sovereign state, counterfeiting has at various times been punishable by death. The practice requires so much skill that only the most expert craftsmen can hope to make dies or printing plates capable of running off coins and currency of acceptable quality. The usual amateurish efforts of the average criminal are not good enough to keep him in business for any length of time. He is doomed.

Educational campaigns to teach collectors to spot counterfeit or altered coins should do much to prevent acquisition of spurious items that have in some way come on the market. Many of the phony "rarities" are very deceptive; others are easily detected by an experienced numismatist. A close examination will disclose from two to a dozen slight or distinct irregularities that finally show the fake coins for what they really are. Source and price of such coins may be important clues to their origin.

Some of the most difficult fakes to recognize are the out-and-out counterfeits that have been made from scratch by casting or die methods. In many cases they are almost too attractive to be genuine, frequently being over-colored or too freshly coined to match the real items that are sought. However, a careful examination under a glass will reveal numerous discrepancies in lettering and various shifted positions of the principal emblems, etc. In all authentication efforts it is important to work with a genuine coin for comparison. Usually a three-power glass is adequate for spotting the variations.

The general furor over counterfeit coins has reached such proportions that the commotion has tended to limit activity in a few issues known to have found favor with the fakers. Complacency and failure to follow through with strong punitive action doubtless have done much to embolden the questionable vendors who may go from place to place until they succeed in marketing both counterfeit and altered coins.

Some experienced collectors and dealers occasionally brush off the suspicious sellers with the statement that the coins are not needed or do not meet certain standards, when they do not wish to become involved in a controversy. It takes quite a bit of courage to tell a man offering questionable coins that he appears to be selling counterfeit or altered items, and especially so where there is a good chance they are genuine. However, the grapevine route usually starts working and news spreads rapidly when doubtful coins are being offered for sale. In this way it may be possible to isolate or quarantine the suspicious seller until the items are verified. In many instances the Secret Service has been called in quickly to do an inspection job the average collector or dealer is afraid to do because of the liability angle. The counterfeiter generally operates under distant or difficult conditions that do not permit use of phones on the spot.

Actually the counterfeit aspect is a very minor one in total numismatics and should not stand in the way of the collector who expects a certain number of surprises in his hobby. The wide publicity resulting from the arrest of a counterfeiter or alteration sharpster is well warranted and doubtless serves as a deterrent to other illegal activities. And so the unsuspecting young collector goes merrily on his way with purchases of such scarce coins as he may need. It is not unusual for the advanced collector to question rare coins offered at prices considerably below the market, and he is the one who frequently puts the finger on the counterfeiter.

The dealer who is offered questionable coins should immediately tell the seller that he thinks the items are not genuine. This certainly does not suggest or impose a liability of any kind, and such a statement should serve as a check on efforts of the seller to dispose of the coins until their genuineness is established. The counterfeiter who is confronted with definite doubt on the part of a collector or dealer will almost invariably leave the premises in a hurry under some unreasonable pretext.

One master counterfeiter actually sold a large collection of spurious ancient coins to the Czar of Russia, who must have been an avid collector without adequate technical advice. It was reported that the same counterfeiter was so expert and productive that galleries and curators once considered offering him a retainer or retirement fund to stop his flood of phony output, proving that talent misused is a dangerous tool.

Many of the most famous collectors were wealthy persons who were not technically inclined, and were willing purchasers of superb counterfeits. In some cases the groups of genuine coins became so mixed with the copies that the identity of both was lost.

Counterfeiting of ancient and medieval coins was so prolific and expert around 1800 that even collectors of today are wary of the bright, uncirculated rarities offered from various unauthenticated sources. Some rare coins displayed in good faith by museums may be spurious, according to experienced numismatists who have studied activities of the master counterfeiters of the past. The same could apply to large private collections, where they have been handed down from one generation to another.

The counterfeiters of the 1800s apparently went so far as to use ancient silver in their copies. This was acquired by melting cheaper ancient coins, or perhaps tableware and bric-a-brac of that period. In some cases the spurious coins appeared too freshly minted, but their beauty more than offset any doubt that lingered in the minds of the purchasers. The sellers usually insisted the coins had come from new-found hoards.

A French counterfeiter was such a skilled engraver that his bogus currency actually was better than the genuine notes. The authorities were able to detect his work from its quality, not its flaws. The faking of both coins and currency so intrigued some of the forgers that they considered the fraud as a challenge; at least to the extent that they wagered considerable amounts they could produce acceptable copies. Use of high engraving skill and an artist's touch gave a few gullible collectors some near-perfect counterfeits that have been a source of annoyance until this day.

About 1955 a large number of magnificent ancient Greek coins appeared in this country. They were in silver and possessed a sharpness unequalled by any that had been found before. They were mostly sold to collectors as genuine, and they could have been.

It was the habit of certain kings or rulers to counterstamp the coins of other countries to make them more acceptable as legal tender in their own small countries. This was mostly done with silver coins of known weight and fineness, and usually the monarch's fancy punch mark was applied. Our own dollars and half dollars were counter-stamped by the ruling regimes of a few small nations, and many of these coins have become rather rare. Counterfeiters have been known to add the counter-stamp to such old coins to make them look like originals and some are very deceptive. Usually these recently punched coins show a "rawness", while others are aged rather cleverly. More will be told later about attempts of fakers to make new counterfeit coins look old.

Although counterfeiting of currency gets most of the publicity, bogus coins are lower in denomination and are not reported to authorities as frequently as they should be. They are found in parking meters, coin machines of low sensitivity, and in places where small change is handled casually. In all frankness it cannot be said that counterfeit coins in denominations from the half dollar to the 1-cent piece are a serious United States problem, except in the case of rarer dates and mint marks.

The U.S. Secret Service has released several important reports since 1965 on the activities of counterfeiters who made and distributed various scarce U.S. coins with the intention of defrauding collectors of the more advanced type. Among these bogus coins were the 1939-D and 1950-D nickels; the 1909-SVDB, 1914-D and 1931-S Lincoln cents, and key coins of other denominations.

The nickels were available in rolls of 40 and were extremely deceptive. They were struck in a copper-nickel alloy very nearly matching that contained by the genuine nickels. Some of the coins were first offered for sale at large bourses, where dozens of experts were fooled for a time. However, the nickels had a slightly grayish color that contrasted with the brighter appearance of the genuine coins. Some of the tell-tale marks that identified the fake coins were small spots here and there in the metal, lack of sharpness of detail under a magnifying glass, and slightly rounded edges. Stress lines that usually appear on genuine nickels were absent on the counterfeits. The general appearance was excellent.

The 1909-SVDB and 1931-S Lincoln cents have been counterfeited with some success. One possible clue to this fraud is the offering of a large quantity of exactly the same quality — usually uncirculated and attractive in appearance. Rare coins generally don't appear in quantities, yet it is not fair to condemn a full roll of such items before making a thorough check. Some of the most deceptive bogus coins offered in this country supposedly came from Hong Kong, Lebanon, Rome and various European capitols.

And thus we see that counterfeiting of coins remains a serious problem only in the field of the rarer dates and mint marks, at least in this country. The making of bogus common and current coins is very nearly a wasted effort, since the expense incurred and the risks involved more than offset the profits. Rank amateurs in high school and college classes occasionally try their hand at making coins, but usually as a challenge or adventure into the slot machine field. Such efforts usually come to naught for many reasons. The spurious coins have no "ring", feel greasy, and will not work in the more sophisticated vending machines. The lead alloys are particularly easy to spot.

Difficulty in convicting international counterfeiters lies chiefly (1) in their ability to claim citizenship in another country; (2) their brazenness in announcing, when under pressure, that they simply were making copies of the original; (3) contention that any type of marginal "merchandising" is legal in a mere hobby, (4) that they were filling a genuine demand for rare coins at a much lower price. Collectors know that all of these claims are dishonest, because the dilution of genuine coins with phonies is both a legal and moral violation of all monetary codes.

Some of the so-called "copies" are not counterfeits in the legal sense of the word, but they are almost worthless from a numismatic standpoint. Many of the current fakes are labeled as copies in very small letters and should be considered no better than play money. Copies of ancient coins may be legally displayed and sold as such, but United States coins must not be copied under any condition.

The gold-plated nickel of 1883 is back with us again, this time in the role of a culprit that has been both suspect and fraud for 85 years. The Secret Service long viewed this little phony with certain toleration, but it actually has been on the black list for a long time. The 1883 nickel, first year of the "V" issue, was about the size of a $5 gold piece, and when gold plated resembled the more valuable coin. Attempts to pass the plated nickels were common around Western bars, but in the East they did not fare so well.

Recent seizure of a few of these gold-plated nickels by Secret Service agents indicates the Treasury Department does not want to take any chances on further circulation of a doctored coin that never had a right to exist. Actually the spurious coin was regarded almost 100 percent by collectors as an ordinary oddity, not as a real numismatic item. Ownership has been greatly liberalized in the past few years.

One sharp operator reportedly passed a number of these gold-plated nickels in the 1880s, and when hailed into court for his fraud was acquitted on the grounds he didn't say a word on presenting the bogus coins. The fact that he made no claims apparently impressed the jury, even if only from a technical standpoint. The first 1883 "V" nickels minted did not carry the word "cents" on either side, but later in the year the dies were changed to include the necessary wording.

Gold coins of every type — both rare and common — have been extensively counterfeited during the recent World demand for the yellow metal. Although it is possible to detect bogus gold coins with proper study, the fact that they are made from good quality gold bullion certainly can make identification difficult. Color of the metal, lack of certain detail, some variance in weight, imperfect lettering, and weak milling on edges are possible clues for the authenticator. Most of the cast coins may be spotted in a hurry, but those made from dies approach perfection.

When a large number of brilliant, uncirculated gold coins of a single date or type are offered for sale, the prospective buyer should check carefully before buying them. They may be perfectly genuine, but identical gold coins free from scratches and blemishes and with unusual brilliance do not ordinarily come in large numbers.

A few countries have been issuing what they call "restrikes", in an effort to convert gold bullion into a premium medium of exchange. All coins of this type sell or trade at various levels above bullion value. Some are struck in proof condition to enhance further their value and desirability. A few extreme rarities are believed to have been minted by certain European countries, an action that placed in circulation several hundred copies of coins that formerly numbered only in the dozens.

The U. S. $3 gold piece has been widely counterfeited by foreign agents who took advantage of the big demand for this obsolete collector's item. Most of these coins are cast from impressions and are fairly easy to detect. The prospective buyer who is offered a $3 gold piece at a bargain price should immediately become suspicious.

A large number of U. S. $1 gold pieces of questionable origin and quality were released in the late 1950s in and around New York City. They were dated 1853 and 1854 and proved to be counterfeits of good quality. One of the principal distributors was apprehended in Dallas and later convicted in a Federal court. A few of these coins doubtless found their way into collectors' hands and may appear from time to time.

The gold collector should not let the relatively few bogus gold pieces spoil his pleasure. Without doubt the percentage of imitations is so small, when compared with the total available gold coins, that he need only keep a sharp eye out in his dealings. All of the reliable dealers and collectors are working toward elimination of fake items of this kind from normal trade channels.

A few foreign counterfeiters have been copying some of the favorite silver coins of American collectors, and they have done a very good job. Among these are the famous Spanish milled dollar (also known as the pillar dollar, eight reales and pieces-of-eight), a few large pieces of Mexico, and various rare crown size coins of several nations. To make the pillar dollars look real, the fakers have buried them, kept them for long periods in salt water, and aged them by different methods to lend a deceptive color. This old coin is a difficult one to copy, due to the elaborate fields on both sides and the fancy edge. Tourists travelling abroad should deal with reputable shops when attempting to purchase large silver coins that date back to the rare eras.

Perhaps another paragraph should be added on counterfeiting as strictly related to currency. The $20 bill is the favorite denomination with the faker, since it is large enough to make a small purchase and receive a nice amount of change in return. It escapes the close scrutiny that goes with the $100 bill. Most of the counterfeiting processes simply cannot pick up the very small lacy, filigreed ornamentation work carried by the genuine bills. A close examination will show lack of detail and smearing of the ink.

Since the currency collector is mostly interested in the old, scarce bills, it is a fortunate fact that the counterfeiter almost completely stays out of this field.

Coins are altered chiefly to make them more valuable in their new form. These practices consist of changing the dates, mint marks, color, lettering or general appearance of coins that at one time were genuine as struck. Mint marks may be buffed off or added, depending on the requirements of the coins being matched. Removal of a mint mark usually leaves a raw spot, although certain processing of the whole coin may conceal the small damaged portion. Addition of mint marks is especially difficult for many reasons. Under a strong glass the tiny cutting marks usually show, and in many cases the whole process appears to be a patched up job. Fusion of any kind is extremely difficult but it may be tried.

In most cases the genuine coin carries enough of its own peculiarities to cause it to stand out prominently from the fake. The 1937-D 3-legged Buffalo nickel is a classic example of a coin that has a dozen distinguishing features. When the buffalo's leg is filed off of the 1937-D, the faked coin fails by a mile to meet requirements of the genuine 3-legged specimen. Thus the real rarity cannot be copied successfully with the use of another coin.

Changing dates is one of the oldest of all altering practices. It involves such efforts as making a 3 out of an 8, removing a part of a 4 to make a 1, making a 6 out of a 5, damaging a figure in a date for making false claims, etc., etc.

In both the changing of dates and mint marks, artisans of a sort have cut out the entire sides of other coins bearing the desired dates or mint marks; then after cutting out the undesired or corresponding sides of the second coins, have patched together the two sides that give the desired rarities. In simpler words, one side is cut out and replaced with the side of another coin that carries the date or mint mark wanted. This usually is done by an expert who cuts just under the rim of the coin in a manner that permits a tight fit of the inserted side. This type of fraud has been carried out many times by using the obverse (heads) of the 1909-S Lincoln cent and the reverse (tails) of the 1909-SVDB of the same issue.

The recent announcement by a promoter that he had found a large quantity of "mint error" Lincoln cents created quite a stir in numismatics. Presumably these cents had got by the mint inspectors in some manner and would be sold as rather expensive misstrikes. A large number of the cents in question were distributed to collectors all over the country, and soon they were accepted in some respectable circles. The Treasury Department was not happy with the appearance of so many damaged Lincoln cents of one date, and was able to establish through the courts that the coins had been altered after regular minting, by overstriking them in some manner with tools or instruments.

The federal laws relating to altering and changing United States coins were for a time neither consistent nor well defined, as evidenced by the fad that made play pieces and souvenirs out of regularly minted coins. The Treasury Department has been rather lenient toward novelty dealers who have damaged, changed or added to both coins and currency in an effort to sell them as trick items. Good examples are the two-headed and two-tailed Kennedy half dollars, rolled out or elongated Lincoln and Indian Head cents, and the $1 Federal Reserve notes with pictures of Kennedy, Johnson, Mrs. Kennedy, Martin Luther King, etc., etc., cleverly pasted over that of Washington on the obverse side.

The various processes appear rather marginal from a legal standpoint, but doubtless the novelty dealers checked on the laws before cutting, defacing or obscuring parts of the coins or currency. Many coins are offered in cut-out designs, where most of the plain surfaces have been cut away to leave only the principal identifying portions attached to the rims. Actually such coins are altered, if only to make them gifts or souvenirs, but they are sold openly without fraudulent intent.

The Kennedy half dollars are cleverly split and the two heads or tails annealed to form a "matching" coin that enables the owner to win whenever he chooses. Such a novelty coin retails for about $3 and makes a nice conversation piece. It is regarded as a trick item of little numismatic value, and perhaps a harmless phony.

The author receives numerous calls each year from innocent collectors or individuals who have obtained split coins with both sides showing heads or tails. All of these items up to now have proved to be the handiwork of a trickster. Only one of the coins under scrutiny failed to show visual evidence of tampering. The bright coloring indicated it had been silver plated after the patching process was completed.

This chapter on counterfeiting and altering coins has been purposely made rather lengthy, since it represents and exposes one of the few means capable of cheating the young collector in his normal pursuits. Still this is not be be construed as meaning that the practice is common enough to be alarming when compared with the whole of numismatics. It is the exception, not the rule.

The U. S. mint at Philadelphia has installed an expensive Microphobe X-ray machine to detect counterfeit and altered coins on a strictly nondestructive basis. In addition an X-ray fluorescence spectometer and a special flame emission unit of an atomic nature have been added. The Treasury Department has been concerned over the wave of counterfeiting and alteration that has undermined the value of certain coins of known rarity, and is willingly cooperating with associations and individuals who have evidence to offer. Importation of copies of some of our key rarities was discovered only because they were first suspected by expert numismatists, then turned over to proper government agencies for special metallic analysis, weight determination, etc.

Uncirculated coins offered at bargain prices may not be a bargain after all. Local coin dealers are an excellent source of advice when in trouble of this kind.

# CHAPTER SIX

# Learning to Grade Coins

*A Little Wear on These Three Hurts Value*

Condition of a scarce coin is nearly always the prime yardstick of value. The general appearance and state of preservation of any coin instantly tells the experienced numismatist an important story. He sees at a glance that a badly worn coin may not be worth one-tenth as much as one in mint condition, although its inexperienced owner cannot understand why "a coin is not a coin," even with its many imperfections.

When the proud and uninformed owner of a rare coin describes it to you, he almost invariably says, "Oh, it is in good condition." And herein lies an important tale. The unsuspecting owner first doesn't know that "good" condition in reality describes a rather poor coin, and secondly that condition has a very special meaning to the veteran collector.

Pride of ownership can play tricks on the perspective and honesty of a few collectors and dealers who may badly stretch a point when describing condition of coins they have for sale. In a heated bartering encounter, the seller frequently claims a higher grading or condition than the prospective buyer will admit. Both are trying to gain a point, but such arguments only tend to show the importance of condition.

Any non-collector who describes the condition of a coin by phone or mail may unwittingly tend toward outright exaggeration without knowing it. It is because of this fact that no final deals should be made before seeing the coins under consideration. Nicks, cuts and scratches are completely overlooked by the uninformed. Even dealers are hesitant to buy from one another where the finer points of condition are under discussion by mail or phone. Unfortunately some overgrading is done by both dealers and experienced collectors who should know better (and do). The latitude and variance between grades are wide enough to permit pluses and minuses, and some take advantage of this weakness.

Thus the "difference in opinion" on grading can be a poor excuse to obtain the highest possible price for a coin sold by phone or mail. It is much better to grade down a little than to paint too glowing a description. Buying coins unseen is at best a kind of "pig in the poke" deal, and overgrading may lead to return of the unsatisfactory items for refund. Sale of coins by mail offers the buyer full protection, and this fact does much to keep all of us within reasonable bounds. However, the buyer may turn out to be the unreasonable person in the transaction. The return of many coins under various pretextes is hardly justified, and especially so where the buyer has expected too much.

Condition and grading are so interwoven that it is difficult to separate one from the other. But rest assured that bad grading does not change the condition one speck. Reality must eventually win, and usually the overgraded coin ends up in the lap of the original offending seller. A considerable amount of money may be involved in a dispute.

A good example of the effect of condition on the price of a coin is the 1942-D Jefferson nickel. This coin in badly worn condition sells for about 25 cents, yet in choice uncirculated condition brings about $6. The 1936-D Washington quarter in average circulated condition sells for less than $1, while a nice uncirculated specimen commands close to $200. From these extreme price ranges it is immediately obvious that condition quickly separates the novices from the experts, and lifts choice material to lofty heights. Collectors simply forgot to save certain uncirculated coins as they were minted.

Where less than a dozen coins of any particular rarity are known, condition may become of less importance. This is especially true where only the worn specimens are known and the demand is great for one of the coins in *any* condition. However, such a case is a rare exception, and generally speaking condition will remain the prime factor in determining the value of scarce coins.

Rarity first makes a coin valuable, but condition is its principal by-product. The strangest part of all this is that rarity frequently is possible only because of superior condition, as related in an earlier paragraph. A roll of 40 circulated quarters may be bought for $40, yet the same roll in uncirculated condition may bring $8,000.

A tendency has developed on the part of various collectors and dealers to grade the very rare or old coins in a lenient or convenient manner. Frequently an advertisement to sell will read, "Very Fine for this coin," or, "About Fine for a coin of this age and rarity." Actually a rare and expensive coin should be graded more conservatively and accurately than an ordinary scarce coin. The very fact that a coin is old or highly desired does not license anyone to overgrade it. Frequently a half grade or a few small scratches can mean a difference of hundreds of dollars in the value of a coin.

There are set rules for grading most coins and they should be followed religiously. Frequently spots and cuts mar the appearance of a coin, even if it otherwise shows only nominal wear. All such defects reduce the value sharply, and price adjustments must be made. Above all, any unusual markings should be mentioned when selling coins by mail or phone, lest you have them back in your lap. Any intelligent person can learn to grade coins, and as he progresses in the numismatic field this is an absolute necessity.

The 1950-D nickel represents the most phenomenal inconsistency in modern times, at least so far as "condition to value" is concerned. A circulated specimen brings almost as much as an uncirculated coin, a fact that has all the experts talking to themselves. Having been a low issue and with a very large number held out in uncirculated condition, the circulated coins turned out to be even scarcer by the roll than the uncirculated ones. This can happen only a few times in a lifetime.

Coins may be technically of a certain grade, while still bearing marks, cuts, bruises or flaws that reduce their desirability and value. Coins of this kind may be fully graded, provided the injuries or mutilations are described. Some coins are historically struck lightly and will not show full sharpness even when strictly uncirculated. Worn dies or minor mechanical difficulties may have caused such shortcomings.

Coloring and doctoring of coins will be mentioned from time to time in various chapters. These practices probably belong in the chapter on Education, but they seem to run over into almost every phase of numismatics. The effect on the value of a coin that has been tampered with or colored may be pronounced — usually on the down side.

Grading standards vary some, both from the number of grades used and the exact condition suggested for each classification. Starting from the bottom and going all the way to the top, the following grading designations should suffice:

*POOR.* Worn almost smooth or slick, but still identifiable by legend or inscription. Date not required but desirable. Usually a coin of very low value.

*FAIR.* Very badly worn, but with date and a good part of the details showing lightly.

*GOOD.* The coin shows heavy circulation, but the principal details, date and lettering show. The high spots are worn off and some of the lettering may be lost.

*VERY GOOD.* The coin is evenly worn, but all of the principal lettering and major features are plain. Only a part of the smallest lettering may be readable where the design has had shallow dies or the relief is precariously high and exposed. Coins in this classification are not as choice as the name suggests.

*FINE:* The coin shows it has been well circulated, but only the highest parts of the surface are worn down. All features and lettering stand out strongly. The coin gives a pleasing appearance, with a nice edge and rim largely intact.

*VERY FINE.* The coin shows some signs of wear all over, but it is in splendid condition. Small lettering is sharp and designs are pleasing. Protected parts of field show little wear, but all luster may be gone.

*EXTREMELY FINE.* Only slight wear will show on the highest spots. Luster usually found in the lower field areas. A choice coin.

*ABOUT UNCIRCULATED.* The coin seems to have circulated slightly, or has been mis-handled in some manner to represent circulation. Doubt would exist over whether the various marks were made from wear or handling in bags. Many collectors use this classification for uncirculated silver dollars that show heavy bag marks. It also applies to $20 gold pieces that have been handled carelessly in bags.

*UNCIRCULATED.* These coins are exactly as minted and never have been distributed for circulation. They are in the "mint" state and show absolutely no wear. However, larger coins develop small cuts and bag marks while being shipped from the mint to distribution points. Some of the bruises and marks are conspicuous.

*PROOF.* Proof coins are specially struck on highly polished planchets for collectors and exhibition purposes. The surface shines like a mirror. They will pass at face value but are rarely spent as ordinary money. The so-called "proof sets" are issued by many countries as a symbol of something special in numismatics.

A great deal of practice and thought is required to make a quick decision on the correct grading of a coin. The tendency to overgrade should be controlled where there is doubt about the finer points of condition. One of the quickest ways to sell a coin is to undergrade it slightly, a strategy that nearly always impresses the buyer. Where a coin is midway between grades, use of the lower grade is especially effective. It is perfectly fair to add "plus" or "minus" to the grading where the coin falls well between classifications.

The new collector is lost in a maze of technicalities when he attempts to describe and grade coins. A few good lessons will straighten him out, while use of grading books also will be very helpful. Just as cotton is sold as "middling", "strict middling", etc., coins should be just as carefully graded.

Many collectors seems to live in a false paradise — in a harmless way, of course. They overgrade their coins through ignorance or pride in ownership, then feel hurt when a dealer or seasoned collector tells them their coins in supposedly uncirculated condition are cleaned, polished or artificially toned in some manner to deceive the novice who has not learned to appreciate the value of true mint luster. Actually such owners have lived mostly to themselves and have taken the word of sellers.

Recently a stranger in a big city called the author and announced he had a large collection of coins for sale. He had been accumulating the U. S. issues for 40 years in his own way and had put together a large number of gold coins, complete sets with all dates and mint marks, type coins, proof sets, rolls, silver dollars and a few thousand odds and ends. The man had started with coins picked from circulation, but had graduated to the buying of necessary scarce coins to complete various U. S. issues.

But there was just one flaw in the whole deal. The poor man had never learned to grade properly, and had acquired a wide range of coins as strictly uncirculated; when they were plainly worn on the high spots, had been severely cleaned, highly buffed, or colored in some manner to conceal slight wear. The collector had become an avid collector of the scarce coins in every stage of condition, mostly through mail purchases, but gullibility was a part of his makeup.

Such an easy-going accumulator derives a great deal of pleasure from coins by living in a happy but deceptive world. He frequently is jarred into reality when he gets old or attempts to get close to "catalog" for the worn Mercury dime, Buffalo nickel and Lincoln cents sets he has formed over the years. He finally sells for the best price he can get, a total usually much less than his original asking price. Suddenly his grading world opens up and he realizes he has accepted overgrading that should have been obvious.

Where the collector has had the courage to grade and price realistically and has remained largely with desirable type and uncirculated coins of all issues, he usually gets top dollar for his collection in any competitive market. Choice coins have advanced spectacularly in the past 15 years and collectors with an expensive taste have been most rewarded. Yet there is also a place for the collector who generally acquires inexpensive items with the full knowledge that they must speak for themselves.

# CHAPTER SEVEN

# Should Coins Be Cleaned?

*1863 Copper-Nickel Cent*

Many coins may be cleaned effectively, while others would be all but ruined by attempts at improvement. This is perhaps the most controversial of all numismatic practices, since tastes differ so widely on what constitutes a really acceptable coin.

A new collector may greatly admire a "raw"-looking large copper cent that has been severely cleaned, but a seasoned hobbyist would consider such a coin virtually ruined. And so the battle rages on — to clean or not to clean. In any series of coins or medals it is absolutely necessary on occasion to resort to mild cleaning of some kind. However, overcleaning or use of the wrong cleaning agents may prove to be worse than no cleaning.

Where coins have been misused or stored in questionable places, the dates may be obscured and the finer details lost to dirt and oxidation. Frequently copper and nickel coins have been varnished or treated, and some type of restoration is fully justified.

In such cases the coins may or may not clean to advantage, but since they were not acceptable in the first place no real harm has been done. Many calculated risks must be faced, but the value of the items involved may be the deciding factor.

Copper coins are the most difficult to clean effectively. Olive oil may be used safely as a rule, yet in the case of proofs and certain uncirculated coins it may damage the sheen. Strong copper cleaners leave coins raw and unattractive to the veteran collector. They should be used sparingly and as a last resort.

In all cases it is better to retain the original luster of uncirculated coins if possible. A pleasingly dark circulated coin should not be cleaned with harsh abrasives or chemicals that will materially lighten its color. When using commerical cleaners make sure they are mild enough for the purpose. Copper coins are very sensitive to any rubbing action, while acids may remove all of the original or acquired appearance.

Where rare old copper coins have been in a fire or have been attacked by some form of deterioration, severe cleaning may be necessary to bring out dates and detail. Even a pencil eraser may help, where such a practice would ruin a nicer coin. When in doubt gradually increase the intensity of action toward the danger point. Some rare large cents came to light in the New England states, following residential fires. Many were damaged almost beyond the point of recognition, while a few show dates and most of the detail.

Nickel coins are rather stable but the early dates are subject to a type of pitting and rust that is impossible to remove. Silver cleaners are fairly effective on circulated nickels dated after 1912, as are a few of the better commercial cleaners. Strong abrasives are ruinous, except in the case of corroded coins with dates obscured, etc. Nickels kept in a dry place will hold their luster permanently. Ammonia and olive oil are good fresheners, while a light touch of ordinary soda may liven worn nickels. Alloys used in nickels occasionally showed unstable elements, or at least those coined around 1870 did. Rust attacks that reflected presence of iron were reported.

Opinions differ sharply over the need or acceptability for cleaning silver coins. Oxidation is the natural enemy of silver and it leaves a dark and mottled tone to nearly all coins in time. Many collectors choose to go along with oxidation rather than gamble with its removal, while others lean toward keeping silver coins on the bright side. Cleaning of circulated coins represents a nominal risk if handled properly.

A complete set of uncirculated commemorative silver coins (U.S.)

will sell about as well in a toned condition as in a bright, obviously cleaned state. Where a collector is able to "see through" oxidation to his satisfaction, he usually accepts it. Some of the fussy veterans would not think of removing the heavy coloring from the older coins, while most of the newer collectors like the bright coins after a gentle cleaning.

The weak cyanide solutions have been used effectively for cleaning silver and gold coins, but they represent a very hazardous process not recommended for collectors. In the case of proofs and uncirculated rarities in silver, cleaning of this kind removes a tiny amount of metal with each cleaning and may soon give the coins a scrubbed appearance. Softness is a fine quality and should be preserved if possible.

Some of the very old, circulated silver coins carry a dark, undesirable coating that will yield only to mild abrasives, such as silver polish. Cleaning in such a case is a rank gamble. Baking soda, cream of tartar or toothpaste may improve certain silver coins that have been mistreated, but they should not be used on the choicer coins.

Silver is admittedly a soft, satin-like metal but it is rather unstable in polluted air or near salt water. Keeping coins of this metal well wrapped in a dry place will pay dividends to the collector who really wants to avoid the cleaning temptation.

Many silver coins are offered as strictly uncirculated when they are well covered by oxidation. The coloring may be extensive enough to cause doubt, and the buyer should insist on some type of determination to establish condition. Cleaning may reveal signs of wear that had been hidden around the edges by discoloration. One collector paid $400 for a rare coin that apparently had an attractive "patina", but dipping in a weak cyanide solution (often called jeweler's dip) melted off the oxidation and scum and displayed a circulated coin worth only $100. No refund was obtained.

Gold is the most stable of all coin metals and is cleaned with various agents from commercial cyanide solutions (dips) to baking soda. Overcleaning is the general rule and should be avoided. Gold coins may take on a kind of fuzziness in time from handling and dust, but the metal itself is unchanged. Slight rust spots and stains from alloys may appear and many are hard to remove. It is difficult to "spot" clean gold coins. Cyanide solutions are dangerous to use.

Mint-condition gold coins usually have a soft, velvety appearance that should be retained at all costs. A new collector once cleaned a gem Roman numeral double eagle, only to come out with a bright, raw coin with the original sheen gone. The scarce coin was damaged by 25 percent in the slight rubbing action.

Circulated gold coins may be cleaned with household ammonia, soda, toothpaste, cream of tartar and various commercial dips. Experience will soon teach the collector when and how to clean gold coins having varying degrees of wear. The chief aim is to avoid a scrubbed appearance that gives a high brightness or slight abrasion.

Gold is one metal that cleans for what it really is. There is no way to make the coins better than they are, but some improvement may be achieved with proper cleaning. The author once purchased a hoard of gold coins that had been buried in the backyard of a country home for 40 years. Just prior to death the old lady asked her children to dig in a certain spot under the door step. They did so and found about 75 gold coins of all denominations in a container that had deteriorated. After the coins were purchased from the heirs through their bank, it was necessary to remove the caked clay from them with a hard scrubbing. A soft brush and laundry detergent finally did the job, but certain stains remained as a reminder of their long contact with the earth. Abrasives would have removed all of the coloring but the gold coins would have been too bright and raw for best appearance.

A few practical examples of cleaning should be listed to assist the collector who may obtain coins in questionable condition, in spite of the fact that many collectors run a high temperature over very dark coins that supposedly have aged "beautifully."

Where a complete set of commemorative U. S. half dollars is obtained, it is possible that some will be bright and clean, others in various degrees of toning, and a dozen or so will have turned almost black. The average collector hardly knows what to do with such a set of 48 or the full set of 142. The bright and dark coins clash in color, since some have been dipped and others have never been cleaned at all. Perhaps half of such owners would lightly clean all of the half dollar to achieve a matching effect, while the other half would permit each coin to find its own color. In all fairness to those holding to the dark patina, an evenly cleaned set of commemorative half dollars looks very pleasing to the eye. In this case, cleaning is largely a matter of taste.

On acquiring a large number of scarce Indian Head cents, many will be light, others dark and dirty. Cleaning all of the cents with olive oil and a soft cloth probably will bring the copper coins up to their best appearance. The same treatment would be required for large U. S. cents and the smaller half cents. Abrasives should be avoided.

A few cleaning and coloring processes have been developed as secret formulas used by professionals. Some consist chiefly of coloring schemes, while others require a follow-up with high heat to set and hold the desired effect. These processes particularly apply to copper coins that are doctored to represent uncirculated coins. Some remain stable for a long time, others fade or lose their beauty with streaked and mottled effects.

Proof coins, those mirror-like beauties, frequently turn dark but great skill is required to clean them. Jeweler's dip may be applied sparingly with some success. A proof starts losing some of its brilliance after a few cleanings. Copper proofs are particularly hard to clean, but olive oil has been used where some type of restoration was a requirement. Doubtful or impaired proofs may be identified for what they really are after a good cleaning.

A copper coin that must be severely cleaned to rawness may be improved in color by placing it in an oven for 20 minutes or less at from 300 to 400 degrees Fahrenheit. Place the coin in a pyrex bowl if possible and keep a close watch on it. Some collectors first treat copper coins with a sulphur solution or salve before heating them. The whole process is a rank gamble, and at best the treated coins pass as circulated items.

CHAPTER EIGHT

# Scarce Coins
# Still in Circulation

*1955 Franklin Half Dollar*

Thousands of requests have been received from collectors who want to know about their chances of finding scarce and even rare coins in circulation. Since the search mostly involves looking through a large number of face-value items, many of our enthusiasts insist they can lose only their time if they fail to find any worthwhile coins.

All of us poke fun at the "strippers", as we call the cullers who spend their weekends looking through roll after roll of coins obtained at the bank or cafeteria. But there are many scarce coins left in circulation, and they keep turning up for the persistent searchers who won't give up. The really good ones are even scarcer than hen's teeth, but where the stripper is tying to find all of the dates and mint marks in such recent series as Jefferson nickels, Roosevelt dimes, Washington quarters and Franklin half dollars, he may eventually complete his sets from circulation. But it takes a lot of patience to do it. Most of these complete circulated sets are not very valuable, but they do command premiums well over face value and represent a triumphant feeling for the searcher.

The really brave collector is the one who tries to find complete circulated sets of Lincoln cents, Buffalo nickels, Mercury dimes, Standing Liberty quarters or Liberty Walking half dollars. The chances are so remote that it would be better during any extended stripping and culling action to hold out all circulated coins with bona-fide premiums on them, than to concentrate on finding the rare dates that are almost non existent.

The green collector who enters the culling field before giving considerable study to the worthwhile recent coins to hold out, usually takes everybody's word on what really constitutes a premium coin.

One adviser will say, "Oh, just hold out all circulated coins minted before 1950." Another will caution the beginner to keep only the mint-marked coins issued prior to 1956. Still a third collector will specify certain scarce coins in the late series that should be saved.

As the result of too much advice, the novice starts holding out as many marginal coins as he can with the hope they will command a small premium by the roll. This may be only a hopeful thought, but again the neophyte reasons to himself that the coins only cost face value anyway. So what the heck! Any coin over 20 years old that has seen little wear is a temptation to the stripper, and especially so if it carries a mint mark. The slick ones of the same dates hardly ever carry premiums. Heavy wear can make a low-premium coin almost useless.

Coin values move so fast that a constant revision of the desirable dates and mint marks must be maintained. The recent circulated coins that would have been completely ignored in 1955 may now carry high premiums. At that time the stripper would have thrown aside dozens of mint marked coins dated in the 1940s and early 1950s that now are in good demand even by the roll. The big coin boom after 1955 brought into demand ordinary circulated coins of many dates and mint marks that were badly needed to fill out sets. This was particularly true of the Lincoln cents, Buffalo nickels, Roosevelt dimes, Franklin half dollars and Jefferson nickels. In fact, this was the big market rush that started more than 10 million people as coin collectors of a sort. They became aware of the chance to search long and hard through coins by the thousands and finally come out with many rolls of coins worth much more than face value. From 1962 until 1965 it was possible to sell circulated rolls by the ton, at least with some kind of premium. The bubble did burst a bit in 1965, but most collectors found consolation in the fact that they had only face value in the coins remaining as a residue. The eager accumulators had been culling the coins too avidly with the hope they couldn't do anything wrong, but the constant fear they might throw away something of value caused them to keep even the very common ones.

The search for scarce and rare coins frequently takes a two-pronged approach by many anxious collectors who seem to dream of smoking out all kinds of rarities. They look through bank rolls every week, and many even make trips to remote areas with the hope the coins in circulation there have more or less been held in a captive state for long periods. Rural districts in the deep South, small towns in the East and West, the Maine woods, and Wyoming ranching areas have been used by numerous collectors who could afford to travel extensively. These also are the persons previously mentioned who never stop asking in every remote county seat town about the presence of coin hoarders.

Hundreds of elderly people, shut-ins and prospectors have looked through bank rolls of ordinary coins seven days per week, but with varying success. Up to 1955 many really scarce coins could be found and some of the strippers did very well. The most successful of the lot planned well and returned the common coins to the bank. However, what was an undesirable coin 15 years ago now is on the preferred list. This, by way of repetition, further emphasizes the necessity for keeping close track of marketable coins that may still be around. Definite information on coins with a potential will follow.

Thus we see there are two principal methods for finding scarce and rare coins still known to be outstanding. The first is simply by looking through the coins we are able to get in rolls or in quantities from banks, stores, parking meters and vending machines. The second involves contact with the constant stream of old coins emerging from estates and discoveries in bureau drawers, bank boxes, etc. Occasionally buried hoards are uncovered from the ground, but the grand rush to the scene by collectors is enough to discourage the average person from becoming part of the scuffle for an advantage.

Indian Head cents have completely vanished from everyday circulation, and with their going we lost a good source of scarce and rare coins. However, there are thousands of small hoards of these cents in homes everywhere, and it is well to keep asking here and there for them. A common Indian Head cent in average used condition will sell for about 29 cents, while the prices range upward rapidly to $50 for the really good ones. The 1877 date brings about $350 in choice condition as a circulated coin.

Prior to 1930 tellers in large banks frequently held out Indian Head cents for customer collectors. In one week as many as 100 might turn up in general circulation. Collectors were then paying about two cents each for the coins in ordinary dates. They have disappeared from circulation for all practical purposes.

About 1875 a fad in the East was the using of Indian Head cents as ornamental buttons for both mens' and womens' jackets. Recently in Dallas a non-collector inherited a large number of these cents in all conditions, along with more than a dozen of the coat buttons encased in brass. Some of the buttons were made from 1869, 1871 and 1872 Indian Head cents in superb condition. Fortunately the cents were only cradled in the brass shells and had not been damaged at all. The whole bunch of cents and buttons brought about $1,100 from a dealer who especially wanted the buttons as they were.

And so we see that old trunks, attics, bureau drawers and safe deposit boxes are still prime sources of scarce and rare coins. A surprisingly large number of families can produce varied assortments of old large cents, half cents, half dimes and gold pieces of every denomination. The demand has been so great that many retired and casual travelers are making a kind of business of the big search for coins, as previously stated. Some of these hunters show remarkable patience and a great deal of skill.

In many cases the scarce coins to be found in estates today were assembled from 40 to 75 years ago by real collectors who knew exactly what they were doing. Usually the heirs know little about coins, and the result is a wild scramble for the residue by dealers and collectors who know or suspect the deceased left a valuable coin collection. Some of the executors are easy to deal with; others hold out for the highest possible prices. In such a case it is not unusual for the rare pieces to bring full catalog prices.

All collectors and dealers dream of finding a hoard of rare coins that can be bought at a low price — a kind of utopia. But most uninformed owners are suspicious and check carefully before selling anything. Some will not sell at any figure for fear of being cheated. In attempts to buy coins encountered in homes, etc., it is better to offer a fair price in the beginning and stick with it than to dicker toward a higher basis.

One of the rarest of all United States coins is the Stockton, California, gold half eagle of 1850. It was found by a San Francisco collector and dealer in the hands of a street peddler. Now valued at $16,000, the Pioneer gold piece undoubtedly had lain in an old Bay City home until released by a maid or some trick of fate. This simply shows that rare coins may appear at any time, but the odds are against it for any one person.

The collector or dealer who conducts a diligent search or advertising campaign will ultimately find valuable coins in homes, estates, etc. There is no guarantee that such a search will prove profitable, yet the chances of uncovering such items as a 1909-S Indian Head cent, nice commemorative coins, scarce dates of old and obsolete items, gold pieces, etc., are good. Most clues turn out to be mere rumors but some are both substantial and lucrative. It is not recommended that collectors turn Gypsy-like and strike out across the country in a big search for the end of the rainbow!

Sensational advertisements of promoters who offer to pay fabulous prices for certain listed rare coins that probably do not exist in general circulation are based, as a rule, on some doubtful motive. Such a dealer usually has something to sell the collector on the spot, generally a catalog or price list at what appears to be a very low price. One dealer over a 50-year period sold perhaps a million coin catalogs to trusting collectors who were looking for 1913 Liberty nickels, 1804 silver dollars and other excessively rare coins that simply never were found in such a manner. The advertiser also was able to buy millions of dollars worth of rare coins from the resulting correspondence. His approach was strictly legal but the contents of his ads were a bit glowing. Most of the current advertisers stay within the realm of good taste.

To any collector who wishes to keep a sharp eye out for scarce coins, it is well to know that most of those he will handle will be of fairly recent origin. This means he must be prepared to flag any of certain scarce or desired coins on his list as they appear. Many novices look at every coin in their purses before spending them, a practice as good as any where the wanted coins are remembered on sight. It is not good taste to approach the bus driver or the milkman and ask him for all of his dimes, cents or nickels. He may be short on some denominations himself.

Some vending machine companies sell their coins to collectors in bulk form at a small premium, claiming they have not been numismatically touched. It is quite a thrill to pour out a gallon or two of coins on a table for culling. It has been impossible to get an acceptable report from collectors on the merits of such a large purchase of unpicked coins, and especially so since the 90 percent silver coins have largely gone into hoarding. Prior to 1966 vending machine companies charged a premium of five to perhaps 10 percent above face value for coins as they were dumped from counting machines, but during the height of the silver-hunting season prices varied even more. Theoretically, scarce coins could be present in vending machine receipts, but to what extent over those obtained at the bank would be difficult to determine.

One of the best tests to determine whether a coin in circulation is worth holding out involves the ability of the finder to sell such coins by the roll on a ready market. Let us say that the coins in question are Lincoln cents in 1949-S, 1951-S and 1955-S. Any one of these coins could be sold by the roll at some kind of premium and doubtless would be held out by the searcher. Occasionally a 1938-S and 1939-D date would appear, and certainly these coins would be kept as a bit scarce and salable by the roll.

The badly worn Lincoln cents of 1916, 1917, 1918, 1919 and 1920 (without mint marks) are barely worth saving, although they are rather old. Such dates as the 1922-D, 1924-D, 1926-S and 1931-D are eagerly sought as scarce coins with nice values. Sprinkled among the Lincoln cents are many with high values and they will be discussed briefly as a general guide for the casual stripper who loves the excitement going along with the hunt.

Scarce and rare United States coins still unaccounted for and believed outstanding should be divided into two distinct groups. The first group consists of those old and perhaps obsolete coins that would *not* be found in circulation, but rather in very old collections and estates that have been handed down for several generations. These are still possible to find in one way or another, but certainly not from bank rolls, etc. A representative list of the very old and rare coins that could turn up follow:

| Coin | Approximate Value in Very Fine Condition |
|------|------------------------------------------|
| 1793 Large cent, chain type | $1,700 |
| 1793 Large cent, with strawberry sprig | *20,000 |
| 1802 Half dime | 4,000 |
| 1876CC Twenty-cent piece | *15,000 |
| 1827 Quarter dollar | *12,000 |

 (Continued on next page)

| | |
|---|---:|
| 1853O Half dollar, without arrows and rays | *30,000 |
| 1873S Half dollar, no arrows | *25,000 |
| 1884-1885 Trade dollars | **15,000 |
| 1834 $2.50 gold piece, with E. Pluribus Unum | 2,000 |
| 1841 $2.50 gold piece, without mint mark | **20,000 |
| 1875 $3.00 gold piece | **30,000 |
| 1879-1880 $4.00 gold pieces | **30,000 |
| 1822 $5.00 gold piece (if uncirculated) | *75,000 |
| 1828 $5.00 gold piece (if dated over 1827) | 3,000 |
| 1798 $10.00 gold piece, with 7 x 6 stars | 3,400 |
| 1915S $50.00 gold piece, octagonal | 12,000 |
| 1915S $50.00 gold piece, round | 14,000 |
| 1815 $5.00 gold piece (if uncirculated) | 10,000 |
| 1819 $5.00 gold piece | 10,000 |
| 1795 $5.00 gold piece, large eagle | 3,000 |
| 1870CC $20.00 gold piece | 20,000 |
| 1804 Silver dollar (original) | 125,000 |
| 1870S Silver dollar (if uncirculated) | 25,000 |
| 1873CC Silver dollar | 1,400 |
| 1889CC Silver dollar | 125 |
| 1893S Silver dollar | 350 |

*Based on estimates          **Proof condition

Admittedly the above prices are a bit on the fantastic side and represent some of the highest priced coins thought to be outstanding. Yet hundreds of additional old coins could have been added to the list, as those also having extremely high premium values. It is well to remember that *any* United States coin more than a hundred years old, if in collectible condition, will add materially to a collection. All of the early cents, half dimes, dimes, quarters, etc., etc., are salable at good prices, if not too badly worn. A good coin catalog is indispensable for determining values and degrees of rarity, just in case the collector should stumble on to something really good.

A second group of scarce and rare coins includes hundreds of various denominations issued since 1900 and known to be in circulation or hidden away in small batches. These are the dates and mint marks eagerly sought by the cullers who constantly look through rolls, vending machine receipts and purses. Coins in this group usually are found in rather worn condition, probably in the grade called Fine or less. For this reason the worn coins are worth only a fraction of the same coins in uncirculated condition. But they are well worth saving and help fill in the various sets or runs greatly desired.

For the casual collector who is looking for premium coins in circulation, the following list is representative of those items he would hold out:

| Coin | Approximate Value in Fine Condition |
|------|-------------------------------------|
| 1909S Lincoln cent | $ 20.00 |
| 1909SVDB Lincoln cent | 100.00 |
| 1911S Lincoln cent | 8.00 |
| 1912S Lincoln cent | 5.00 |
| 1914D Lincoln cent | 45.00 |
| 1922 Lincoln cent | 3.00 |
| 1924D Lincoln cent | 8.00 |
| 1926S Lincoln cent | 3.00 |
| 1931S Lincoln cent | 20.00 |
| 1955 Double die Lincoln cent | 175.00 |
| 1960 Small date Lincoln cent | *2.50 |
| Liberty or "V" nickel (any common date) | 1.25 |
| 1912S "V" nickel | 42.50 |
| Buffalo nickel (any common date) | .20 |
| Buffalo nickel (several early dates) | 20.00 |
| Buffalo nickel (common early dates) | 4.00 |
| Buffalo nickel (most common early dates) | 2.50 |
| Buffalo nickel (best of dates in 1920s) | 20.00 |
| Buffalo nickel (common dates in 1920s) | .50 |
| 1931S Buffalo nickel | 4.00 |
| 1937D Buffalo nickel (3-legged variety) | 40.00 |
| 1938S Jefferson nickel | 2.00 |
| 1939D Jefferson nickel | 3.00 |
| 1950D Jefferson nickel | 7.50 |
| 1951S Jefferson nickel | .40 |
| 1955 Jefferson nickel | .40 |
| Jefferson nickel (various mint marks) | .25 |

 (Continued on next page)

| Coin    Approximate Value in Very Fine Condition | |
|---|---|
| 1916 Mercury dime | 225.00 |
| Mercury dime (certain early dates) | 4.00 |
| Mercury dime (average early dates) | 3.00 |
| Mercury dime (common dates before 1930) | 1.00 |
| Mercury dime (most common dates) | .25 |
| Barber or Liberty quarter (certain early dates) | 200.00 |
| Barber or Liberty quarter (medium early dates) | 6.00 |
| Barber or Liberty quarter (common dates) | 1.50 |
| Barber or Liberty quarter (scarcest) | 500.00 |
| 1916 Standing Liberty quarter | 470.00 |
| Standing Liberty quarter (scarce early dates) | 30.00 |
| Standing Liberty quarter (medium early dates) | 12.00 |
| Standing Liberty quarter (common early dates) | 8.00 |
| Standing Liberty quarters (late common dates) | 3.00 |
| 1932 (S or D) Washington Quarter | 45.00 |
| Washington quarter (certain early dates) | 2.00 |
| Barber or Liberty half dollar (rare early dates) | 60.00 |
| Barber or Liberty half dollar (many scarce dates) | 30.00 |
| Barber or Liberty half dollar (any date) | 22.00 |
| Liberty Walking half dollar (rare early dates) | 75.00 |
| Liberty Walking half dollar (medium scarce dates) | 25.00 |
| Liberty Walking half dollar (any date) | 1.25 |
| Franklin half dollar (certain scarce dates) | 5.00 |
| Franklin half dollar (certain dates) | 1.50 |
| Franklin half dollar (any date) | 1.35 |
| 1964 Kennedy half dollar | 1.60 |
| 1964 Kennedy half dollar (as graded above) | 1.35 |

*Uncirculated

There are so many scarce coins dated after 1900 that the above list merely serves as a guide toward a more complete group. Nearly all of the Lincoln cents with mint marks that are dated before 1930 have at least a minimum premium, and especially those prior to 1920. The same condition prevails with nickels, dimes and quarters. Anyone interested enough to search through large quantities of current coins certainly will equip himself with adequate lists. Where he draws the line is his own business.

In 1956 a collector looked through 3,000 cents over the weekend and was able to find coins with a premium value of about $6.00. The next weekend he took home 50 rolls, or 2,000 nickels, from which he found coins with a premium value at that time of about $7.00. The reward hardly paid for his work, except that he enjoyed every minute of the careful search. The current prices of the coins held out in 1956 are much higher than those prevailing at the time of the weekend hunts. In fact, small premiums are appearing each year on groups of coins that carried no premiums previously. This natural enhancement is caused by age and scarcity that develops in spots.

For the casual collector who loves to scan coins as a part of the hobby, he may be able to obtain the receipts of cafeterias, washateries, various vending machines, parking meters, etc., in his quest for the scarce items. Shut-ins and many elderly people become avid collectors by using every available source open to them. The temptation is to hold out coins of questionable value, and especially so because they are mostly obtained at face value.

# CHAPTER NINE

*U.S. Proof Sets in Special Holder*

# Proof Sets and Other Special Issues

Proof coins represent a special type of beauty, art and vanity that go along with numismatics. They are something special as the ultimate for the collector who tends toward a desire for coins worth more than face value at time of coinage. They stand out from common coins because they are made by a luxurious method that places them above the bourgeois of hard money, and therefore something to be saved, not spent casually.

The idea of proof coinage first evolved from an early desire to strike medals, commemoratives and presentation pieces of a better quality and finish than could be achieved with ordinary dies and planchets. The mirror appearance required honing of dies, special treatment of the metal strips or discs and great pressure in striking. The brilliant appearance had to be achieved through the actual minting process, not by buffing or polishing afterwards. The first so-called proofs were the natural result of attempts to strike coins, medals and special pieces of the highest quality.

A proof coin is simply one specially struck on polished planchets, or blanks, for collectors or exhibition purposes. The surface carries a high mirror finish, and all details are strongly developed from the pressure and minting process. Naturally the collector must pay extra money to the mint for these beautiful coins.

Thus we see that proof coins are both face value and premium items from the very beginning. Hundreds of these coins doubtless have been put in circulation since 1860 by children and wives who spent them in a pinch for candy or groceries. Words of the fathers or husbands who owned them are strictly unprintable. Some have turned up in banks, parking meters, grocery stores and post offices as ordinary change. Since they are playthings for finicky collectors, they are mostly kept under lock and key by proud owners.

The enormous number of proof coins issued since 1950 has changed this once exclusive group from an oddity to a commodity — literally. Wide publicity has familiarized the general public with the nature of the coins and the procedure for obtaining them from the mint. "I want to get a few proof sets for my grandchildren," is a kind of standard expression we hear every year. Most of the embryonic buyers expect a steady enhancement in value, while the regular purchasers seem to obtain them as a form of annual habit. Speculators order all they can get with the hope the sets will advance rapidly on the open market.

Proof-making was a sort of fetish with engravers and mint officials long before such coins were offered to the general public. Silver dollars lent themselves especially well to proof coinage, largely because of their extensive field of open exposure. The mint started toying with proof silver dollars in 1836 as transitional pieces, and continued minting them with the regular issue of 1840. The use of steam presses about 1836 also made issuance of proof coins easier, since uniform pressure is a constant aid.

Public interest in proof coins was not extensive until renewal of their coinage in 1936, following a lapse since 1916. Proof coinage was suspended with the 1942 issue, but again resumed in 1950 by popular demand. Evidence of the growing favor of proof sets is graphically shown by the recent spurt in sales to the public by the United States Mint. Totals shown from 1936 through 1942 represent the minimum number of complete sets that could have been formed. Many extras, as "singles", were struck in some denominations.

69

| Year | Proof Sets Issued |
|------|------------------:|
| 1936 | 3,837 |
| 1937 | 5,542 |
| 1938 | 8,045 |
| 1939 | 8,795 |
| 1940 | 11,246 |
| 1941 | 15,287 |
| 1942 | 21,120 |
| 1950 | 51,386 |
| 1951 | 57,500 |
| 1952 | 81,980 |
| 1953 | 128,800 |
| 1954 | 233,300 |
| 1955 | 378,200 |
| 1956 | 669,384 |
| 1957 | 1,247,952 |
| 1958 | 875,652 |
| 1959 | 1,149,291 |
| 1960 | 1,691,602 |
| 1961 | 3,028,244 |
| 1962 | 3,218,019 |
| 1963 | 3,075,645 |
| 1964 | 3,950,762 |
| 1968S | 3,041,509 |
| 1969S | 2,934,631 |

Complete proof sets struck since 1904 have each consisted of the cent, nickel, dime, quarter and half dollar, with a face value of 91 cents. For several years, ending with 1964, the price was $2.10 per set and no limit had been placed on the number that could be ordered, at least within reason. However, the latest 1968S proof set was issued at $5.00, and the limit per order was 20 sets.

The proof set hysteria has been one almost impossible to understand. The millions of sets now available are virtually identical in appearance, yet collectors, accumulators and hoarders cannot seem to get enough of them. They have become a standard commodity and are traded in by the thousands. Sealed proof sets must of necessity be stored and held as expendable items. They do not circulate as ordinary money, draw no interest as such and are mostly retained in original mint envelopes. But any premature assessment of their value five, 10 or 15 years from now might be unfair to the coins as numismatic material.

Many wealthy collectors have invested heavily in proof sets. The demand has run prices upward at various times since 1955. The 1957 proof set that originally cost $2.10 sagged a year later to about $1.80, but it subsequently recovered and has since been quoted at three times its issuing price. Most proof sets for the present are bringing at least twice their original cost, and certainly the author knows no more than other collectors whether they will prove to be a good investment. The neglected sets or singles issued prior to 1940 have proved to be sensational market performers, with the 1936 set of five coins ranking among the best rarities in the whole realm of coin.

The selective, conservative collector of single scarce coins generally steers away from proof sets in quantity. He contends that any coin available by the millions cannot possibly become rare enough to remain in demand, should economic conditions change. To this simple soul, the rush to buy and hoard common coins of any kind is a breach of collecting decorum, yet he has seen many in this group grow valuable in the form of rolls.

But on and on goes the scramble for proof sets — any proof sets. Many dealers are recommending them as an investment. Others warn against buying in quantity, contending that the demand surely will diminish. The matter has not become an impasse by any means but it could. It is felt that a strictly impartial report should be made here in the interest of the proof set cause. As taxes and trends change, proof coins may also vary in appeal. A collector or hoarder with 1,000 sets and a $6,000 investment will sit and wait on his treasure, while hoping for future enhancement. If it does not come, the rarity collector will say, "I told you so."

In the scramble to obtain recent proof sets, the newer numismatist has almost lost sight of the beautiful single proof coins minted from 1855 until 1916. They run very expensive. And therein seems to lie the real difference between a true collector and an accumulator. The early proof coins, as singles or sets, are rather expensive.

The coin shortage in 1964 forced discontinuance of proof sets for three years. In an effort to please collectors the Treasury Department in 1965, 1966 and 1967 issued so-called "special mint sets", a process that actually was a compromise to save time and minting machinery. These special sets consisted of one coin of each denomination then being struck, from the cent through the half dollar. The coins were of better quality than the regular issues, but not as good as the former proofs. Priced at $4.00 per set, the special mint sets were not regarded at time of issue as any kind of special bargain, since the former proof sets of much finer quality had sold for $2.10.

Each year prior to the 1964 coin shortage the Treasury Department had further tried to please collectors by furnishing them with ordinary uncirculated coin sets from the various mints. They were provided at a small premium, enough to take care of handling. This practice has been started again and probably will continue. These mint sets have been the basis for a complete run of uncirculated coins for collectors everywhere, and some of the yearly sets have become rather scarce and valuable.

Proof sets and special coin sets have been issued by many nations, some for primary distribution in this country. Panama, Israel, Canada, South Africa, Great Britain, etc. etc., have made strong efforts to please world collectors with special coinage. Some of these sets have greatly increased in price, others have not. But in all honesty it should be said that where small issues were distributed, collectors have profited from their participation. The true numismatist generally does not consider original issuing prices or the dream of higher values when he acquires proof and other special sets. He gets them because they will add to his collection.

And so we must conclude that the proof set holder has acquired this type of coin for three principal reasons — pleasure, investment and speculation. The collector who has only one set for each year of issue regards them as a small part of his total numismatic interest. The plunger who has several hundred sets watches the market with a view toward profit. The speculator who has no sets at the moment is the one who stands by and wonders what to do about it. The most acceptable plan seems to be one that involves looking at proof sets on the basis of the number issued during certain years.

Commemorative coins of the United States undoubtedly represent the most colorful and classic phase of our long coinage series. They were principally struck to commemorate great historic events, to honor important people and to assist in financing certain patriotic memorials through their sale to the public above actual face value.

Such coins always have been sold at a small premium, in order that the sponsoring commissions could apply the profits to the events being honored. Our mint first assigns the coins at face value to the special commissions, and they are passed on to collectors at an agreed premium. Some of our early commemoratives have been minted in numbers too large for public acceptance, a fact that will be discussed later.

Official commemoratives have been struck only in silver and gold. They range in denomination from the famous Isabella quarter of 1893 to the magnificent $50 gold pieces of 1915. All told, 61 distinct types of commemorative silver and gold coins have been issued by the United States from 1892 to 1954. However, the addition of mint marks, dates and varieties has increased the total mint varieties to 155. Numismatists do not fully agree on the difference between a type and variation in a few cases among this series.

Only 48 distinct types of commemorative half dollars were struck, but for some reason all three mints joined in the procession and a complete set of these half dollars now popularly consists of 142 coins. This means that 94 of the total are exact duplicates of the original 48, except for dates and mint marks.

The minting of commemorative half dollars was badly overdone in spots. They were coined year after year, and all three mints helped create the surplus. The Texas half dollar was coined yearly from 1934 through 1938; the Oregon type periodically from 1926 through 1939, and the Arkansas half dollar from 1935 through 1939. Doubtless the original plan was to coin each commemorative half dollar for one year only, but some of the sponsoring commissions pressed for continued coinage to meet obligations, with a bit of vanity.

Coinage of various type half dollars range from a low of about 10,000 to more than 2,000,000 in some series. The mint was forced to melt down or release at face value a large percentage of certain commemorative half dollars remaining unsold. Some of the unpopular commemoratives that were melted in part now command very high prices. A prime example was the beautiful $50 Panama-Pacific gold commemorative of 1915. It went begging at around double face value, but now it sells well into the thousands of dollars. The Lewis and Clark Exposition commemorative gold dollars of 1904 and 1905 were offered at the Saint Louis World's fair at $2.00 each, but now one will bring around $600.

The importance of rarity in any coin is superbly proved by the low-issue commemoratives. The Hudson, Hawaiian and Spanish Trail types each had a coinage of 10,008, a mere pittance when compared with the number of collectors who want one. These coins are a "must" in any type or complete set and they have been selling in the hundreds of dollars each for several years. At their issuing time they sold with difficulty at a nominal figure above their face value. All of which shows that any attempt to predict a future for any coin is quite a guess. This also supports the former statement that diversification eventually will pay off if the collector uses average judgment.

The 1892 and 1893 Columbian Exposition commemoratives were so over-minted that they finally were released in quantity at face value through banks. They sold in uncirculated condition at about 65 cents until after 1942. Original issuing price was $1.00. However, the influx of millions of coin collectors has created a new and expanded image even for this coin and today it brings several times its issuing price in top condition.

We have issued no commemorative half dollars since 1954, despite a general clamor for one or more. The Treasury Department feels that if the barriers were let down again it would be almost impossible to screen a few really worthwhile commemoratives from the flood of applications that would follow. The mint has been so busy with its regular and proof coinage that commemoratives have appeared far off. But at some time one will be struck, even it should become one honoring the Declaration of Independence in 1976!

The Greeks and Romans struck commemorative coins in both silver and gold, or at least their equivalents. All modern nations issue commemoratives, much as we have done. Many of the first struck exploited the virtues of royalty or situations dear to the throne, while others were in types along the lines of our own. Some were in the form of medals and special monetary issues that eulogized national pride, products and heroes.

And so it is obvious that commemorative coins are a definite part of numismatics. They are beautiful but it is possible they have been overdone in spots. In this country such coins are so basic that they immediately tell their interesting historical tales.

With no intention of straddling the fence, it might be wise to offer a brief summation on proof coins as a whole. They have been numismatic items in the strict sense of the word since 1836 and playthings of a sort since 1790. Starting out as something individual and special, they have grown into a major part of coinage.

Proofs in gold started right along with the silver ones in 1855 and continued without a break until 1916. The demand was so poor during the 1870s and 1880s that during some years less than 30 were struck in certain denominations. The mint apparently kept issuing gold proof to satisfy the handful of faithful collectors who wanted them. It must have cost a lot of money to run off only a handful of these beautiful coins.

The rapid rise in coinage from a few to nearly four million sets has distinctly changed the proof coin picture. Nobody knows how the large issues since 1955 will fare in the future with collectors. Certainly the scarce ones will be in high demand, but those on the plentiful side will have to fend with other coins for future popularity.

Through an oversight no mention of the dull, mat proofs struck from 1908 until 1916 were mentioned. They reflect the French influence of the time and did not last for a long period. Such coins also were known as sandblast proofs. Although a thing of beauty, their dullness never quite caught on with the American fancy.

Medals and tokens will be discussed in another chapter as special issues issued by the mint and private organizations.

# CHAPTER TEN

# Coins As an Investment

Prior to 1950 interest in numismatics was confined to perhaps a million persons who collected coins on the premise they were something to have and to hold. Almost suddenly shortages began to appear in many issues that formerly were lightly regarded. The public heard about this and came into the picture by the millions as collectors, hoarders, speculators and investors. The news media featured coins in bold stories in magazine sections of large daily papers, the national slick magazines told sensational stories of new millionaires via the coin route, while the press services were telling of certain scarce coins still in general circulation. The whole parcel added up to a tremendous increase in coins as something more than mere spending money.

In the early 1950s several of the most astute collectors and dealers in the country started buying uncirculated rolls of coins that previously had attracted little attention. The mintage was low for the year, yet certainly there should have been enough to give each collector at least one coin. But the speculators and investors did not want a single coin; they wanted the low yearly issues by the roll and by the ton if they could get them. They knew that heavy buying would have two principal effects. It would attract attention to the coin, and secondly it might even create a shortage.

Collectors of the old school continue to frown on the increased trend toward speculation in recent coin issues that have little numismatic appeal. These old-timers feel for some reason that the hobby should continue to be one yielding a great deal of fun and very little profit, a stipulation that certainly does not appeal to the wheeler-dealer who wants to make a successful venture of a growing pastime and hobby.

The painstaking numismatist shops around for rarities, while the average collector will gladly acquire what seems to be an ordinary investment for tomorrow. Thus we have the puritanical hobbyist who abhors even the thought toward coins in bulk, versus the avowed speculator and hoarder who continues to make a market for all types of recent uncirculated items with limited potential. Each views the other with some suspicion.

For the moment, bulk sales of such common coins as ordinary silver dollars, proof sets and assorted specialty items like the 1968-S cents and nickels account for a big percentage of total numismatic transactions. The vast expansion of the hobby in all directions has somewhat departed from the old saying, "If you cannot afford the best, buy the best you can afford." The attitude now seems to be that a collector should buy whatever strikes his fancy, a vast trend that has greatly stimulated the hobby.

A recent example of a get-rich-quick coin is the 1950-D nickel, of which 2,630,030 were coined. During the 1920s such an issue would have gone completely ignored, but this coin got caught in the big spiral that lifted all low issues to new heights and much greater respect. One dealer started plugging this nickel from the very beginning, and at one time is said to have owned or controlled the market on up to 2,000 rolls of 80,000 coins. The 1950-D nickel sold at one time for $900 per roll, thus making the dealer a millionaire. This example may be an isolated one in a phenomenal involvement, yet it is one of thousands of instances where investors and intelligent persons saw the demand for low-issue coins before they had a chance to shoot upward from relative obscurity. Admittedly publicity and speculation played prominent parts in attainment of higher coin quotations, but the same condition prevails on stock markets.

In discussing coins purely from an investment standpoint we leave behind many of the hobbyists who claim to be interested only in the numismatic angle. Yet even the most conservative collector will point with pride to price gains in coins owned.

The field of numismatics could have grown so rapidly only because so many less selective collectors, accumulators and speculators joined the parade to make the hobby a kind of business. Until 20 years ago the chief excitement was caused by the purchase of a rare coin for a fabulous sum. Now the availability of a late series by the ton may cause a bigger stir in a different direction. Many of the wealthy have stuck with the rarities, and a single coin may bring more than $10,000.

Despite the orgy of speculation in relatively common material, a really rare coin sells readily. And oftentimes to a speculator who hopes to move it soon at a profit! Finger pointing has no place in buying or selling coins, since the man who risks his money for any given purpose is entitled to the privilege. The thrill of owning a choice United States cent of 1799 apparently should be much greater than the accumulation of $3,000 worth of recent coin rolls, but with many investors and speculators it isn't. The difference in points of view has been the great division that has made coin collecting a grand diversion for so many people. Some want to go about it quietly; others wish to consider it a form of investment.

Only a thin line exists between investment and speculation. And even that line may be largely interpretive. We think of an investment position as one involving quite a period of time, while a speculative venture should see action in less than a year. The father who buys and earmarks certain groups of coins for his children's education *hopes* he is making a good investment. The trader who acquires coins with the view of selling them at a profit in a few months pursues a speculative course. The true investor is not above welcoming any quick gain that comes his way, and frequently he and the speculator unwittingly buy the same series of coins for entirely different reasons. Thus we see that the complexion of a transaction may be based largely on point of view.

What coins should be bought for future profit? Will rolls be a good long-term investment? Will the rare coins keep going higher? Will silver dollars increase steadily in value? Will counterfeiting hurt the coin market on a sustained basis?

Collectors with an eye toward investment write hundreds of letters asking for information on probable trends in the numismatic field. This is only a natural development in a rather hectic hobby that has seen several million people join in the exciting chase for almost any coins that catch the public fancy. But the hobby and business aspects have become greatly confused by the influx of so many mixed and unsure interests.

Danger signals immediately appear when any industry or hobby becomes so expanded, promoted and publicized that it attracts a burst of new and inexperienced capital. In the rush to enter headlong into frenzied activity, patience may be thrown to the winds and the novices singed rather painfully before they get their bearings. Such a danger is present whether the endeavor is uranium mining, wildcatting for oil or the broad field of numismatics. A good rule always is to proceed with at least normal caution.

Many wealthy men who quickly become interested in coins like to take a firm and large stand before investigating all aspects of the endeavor. What is said here may appear somewhat repetitious, but the investor should familiarize himself with the prime nature and possibilities of transactions under consideration. Bankers and professional men have been known to yield unduly to influences striving to rush them in to coin deals favorable to the sellers. Fortunately in the past most of these plungers have come out smelling like a rose, largely because of the great upswing in coin prices since 1955.

Since any thought of investment at this time involves the future, not the past, we find ourselves in the same guessing position as the prospective buyer of General Motors or Texaco. AT&T looks good, we may say, but the growth factor must also be present in the coins we have in mind. The various tried and true performers on the "Big Board" stand out, yet they do not seem glamorous enough for the speculator who wants quick action. Exactly the same picture may be seen in the field of numismatics.

Until 1964 scarcity, condition and to a lesser degree, age, were prime factors in probing around for soundness of position. Now another factor has entered the picture — the quality of the metal in the coin under consideration. Gold and silver have finally broken out of their ruts and are threatening to enter higher price levels. This fact obviously has made silver and gold coins desirable as bulk holdings, rather than face-value items of 40 years ago. And with this change has come a rush for the more precious coins for future markets. The Treasury Department's position on melting will largely determined the future of both silver and gold coins. Millions of dollars were invested in 90 percent silver coins on the theory they would eventually be melted legally into bullion. The premium on U.S. gold coins never has been based on such an assumption.

Each year the various coin publications ask dealers and leading collectors to predict trends for the next 12 months. The result is a giant hodge-podge of guessing and reasoning that is supposedly designed to aid both the collector and investor toward successful portfolios. A check-back at the end of the year usually proves that a high percentage of the forecasters were wrong in their predictions. Being only ordinary human beings, some of the forecasts could have been prompted by hope as much as by conviction. It is not reasonable to assume that a man with a sure-fire investment plan will rush into print to tell the world about it. However, most of the predictions are well-meant and certainly are widely read by the investor looking for a course of action.

The speculation that was responsible for pushing up certain prices to precipitous levels in the past has, in many cases, been equally responsible for holding values of those coins to much higher levels than were expected after the decline from peak positions. In simpler words, the coin roll that originally started upward from a listed value of $20 and finally topped out at $75, usually did not return to its original $20 price, but stabilized on the way down at perhaps $50.

Before investing heavily in coins the collector should review past performances, just as he would study the action of the stock or bond market. This could be accomplished by scanning both recent and old coin catalogs and the basic values that have prevailed over the past 20 years. Future repetition of past actions is in no way guaranteed, but such a study will show the investor (1) items that have consistently advanced, (2) those that have raced ahead on only one major move, (3) issues that have advanced and dropped back on occasion, and (4) those that failed to rise proportionately with the general upswing during the past 20 years. Occasionally a good neglected issue will stand out prominently because of its low coinage or desirability as a type coin.

The recent coins that have not had the opportunity to show market trends naturally will have to be appraised on another basis. They are the newer arrivals that are perhaps available in bulk, just as most were prior to 1955. In this category are the dozens of sleepers that may catch fire from speculation and genuine demand in the future.

Many promising coins have such unusual quirks as deviation from standard design of the past, variation in metals used, scarce mint marks, etc. Among these are the Kennedy half dollar of 1964, the wartime silver nickels, steel cents of 1943 and many others.

Any key or type coin of low issue cannot possibly escape the interest of true numismatists and investors, unless the basic concepts of the hobby change. And they certainly should not shift radically from any deviation now in sight. Therefore, scarce coins of known numismatic appeal should prove the real investments of the future. A longer discussion of scarce, recent rolls will be presented in a later chapter.

But make no mistake about it; choice coins have been an excellent investment since 1950. They are now generally from two to 10 times higher than during 1949, although they have receded from their peak of 1964 in many instances. The market has become rather selective and the common material minted since 1958 does not for many reasons hold the future promise the 1937-1955 issued had. The drop in recent prices, where they did occur, were conspiculously confined to the common coins and circulated rolls that were run up by speculation. However, some of the better coins that were pushed upward out of all reason did back off for various reasons. The next big coin boom may conceivably see quotations on the scarce key coins far above any of those in the past.

The term "investment" is a very flexible one and appears to be largely a matter of perspective and the pocketbook. A grandmother or young collector might consider $500 as a large investment for the long pull. A wealthy plunger might not stop under $100,000 in an effort to tackle the job in a thoroughly diversified manner. Both are grasping for the same supporting premises, but on different magnitudes.

Future trends on coins now available will depend largely on the collecting whims of the public, degree of inflation, gold and silver bullion prices and the growth of numismatics. Every collector should strive to mix enthusiasm with restraint in an effort to cover both the fields of pleasure and profit. Selectivity will be the key to success.

Investing at face value in the recent issues is one sure way to play the game safely — or is it? Putting aside a large quantity of the 1965-68 clad issues with their tremendous coinage would necessitate a gain of about six percent each year in value to offset carrying charges, storage, etc. Due to the debasement of those years, such a plan is not recommended even on a hoarding basis. A few rolls of each denomination would be an excellent inventory, but a thousand rolls do not now sound like an investment.

The following group of coins provide items known to be basic and representative. As the hobby grows, they should participate in any activity tending toward higher prices:

1. Uncirculated sets of all Lincoln cents in two categories; the first from 1934 to Date; the second from 1909 to Date (complete).
2. Uncirculated sets of all Jefferson nickels from 1938 to Date.
3. Uncirculated sets of all Roosevelt dimes from 1946 to Date.
4. Uncirculated sets of all Washington quarters from 1932 to Date.
5. Uncirculated sets of all Franklin half dollars from 1948 through 1963.
6. Any uncirculated sets of issues the investor can afford; such as Mercury dimes, Indian Head cents, Liberty "V" nickels, two-cent pieces, Barber dimes, quarters and half dollars, etc.
7. Nice circulated sets of any of the older issues that are available.
8. Complete sets of silver dollars from 1878 (in both circulated and uncirculated). This might exclude some of the rarest.
9. Silver dollars from 1795 through 1803.
10. Silver dollars from 1840 through 1873.
11. Uncirculated type coins of all issues.
12. Choice circulated type coins more than 100 years old.
13. U. S. commemorative coins in all metals; singles or complete sets.
14. From one to 10 proof sets of all dates since 1949, if within budget.

15. Proof sets before 1950 if budget will permit.
16. Common U. S. and foreign gold coins selling closest to bullion value.
17. Rare U. S. gold if budget will permit.
18. Private and Territorial gold of this country if budget will permit.
19. Colonial and early coinage of this country.
20. Silver crowns of the World. Study this group carefully before investing.
21. Scarce and rare foreign coins in any metal if priced realistically.
22. World proof sets if officially sponsored.
23. Scarce and offbeat tokens of U. S. and other countries.
24. Scarce U. S. rolls selling considerably below their former peak prices; in uncirculated condition unless very expensive as single coins.
25. A mixture of medals if they have been well sponsored and not struck as a purely commercial venture. Avoid medals that may turn out to be nothing more than souvenirs or momemtos.
26. U. S. and Canadian paper money in the older types.
27. Scarce odd money of the World.
28. Any old hoards of coins that can be aquired at attractive prices!!

The author who sticks his neck out with a recommended list of coins should temper his choices with certain qualifications. Groups of coins that have only recently participated in big upswings hardly look as attractive as those that have not yet moved to higher ground. Of course, nobody knows when the top is reached. It may be dangerous to climb on the bandwagon after the promotion is about over.

The smartest investor studies the various coin issues carefully with the view of finding coins that (1) have a low mintage, (2) have not yet boomed in price, (3) have sold consistently as necessary or key coins, (4) have an unusual appeal of some kind (special metal or design), or (5) have a strong appeal as old and obsolete coins.

The safest way is to buy and hold real quality, with the marginal items included as possible leaders.

# CHAPTER ELEVEN

# Sensible Displays, Loose Talk and Theft Prevention

*50 Pesos Mexican Gold,
a Very Heavy Coin*

Proud collectors love to display their coins to friends, to dealers, the public and to anyone who will look and listen. The more elaborate and expensive the collection, the greater is the pride in ownership. In due time practically everybody knows about the prize-winning collections in any given area, with such additional information as the habits of owners, their storage arrangements and the usual number of valuable coins kept around the house. Much of the conversation is only small talk that never generates any trouble.

Of course, all of these details are harmless among average fellow collectors, but a real danger may lie among a certain small group of buddy-buddy aquaintances or strangers who are bent on robbing collectors after casing their intended victims from every angle.

Perhaps coin thefts are no greater percentagewise than those in any other luxury hobbies, but they do occur frequently because of the ability of thieves to know in advance what they are seeking. Some of the hijackers know more about coins than we would suspect, as evidenced by their ability to toss aside the common items in favor of the better ones.

The difficulty in identification of coins works to the advantage of the offenders, a fact that may prevent the owner from swearing positively that recovered coins under questioning are his. In the case of extreme rarities, or where coins bear unusual marks and colorings, positive identification is possible. Small coin envelopes and markings on rolls also are good identifying features, although it is the custom of robbers to dispose of such containers immediately. One large collector secretly marks all of his rare coins in a clever way that ordinarily would never be detected.

The purpose of this chapter is not to alarm, but rather to warn collectors of the danger of flagrant coin displays; and to do so necessitates exposure of tactics used to steal valuable collections under numerous circumstances. Naturally persons with large and valuable collections are more susceptible to thefts than the smaller collectors who are known to own inexpensive items. However, juvenile offenses are frequent where young boys tend to tell their friends all about the coins they keep around the house.

Every advanced collector likes to admire his coins and to classify them at home during his leisure hours. This natural desire has been responsible for many hijackings by thugs who doubtless knew all along that the coins were on the premises.

All well-known coin collectors should beware of the person who appears unexpectedly at the door and yells, "Package for Mr. Jones," — "Special Delivery for Mrs. Jones," — "Telegram for Mr. Jones," or "Collecting for the morning paper."

He may be a stickup man who will tie you up and rob you. And he may even use force in an effort to locate valuable coins you do not have in the house. Most of the time the robber knows the victim's habits and the approximate value of the collection he is after. Once inside he takes it for granted the coins are on the premises.

Coin robberies have increased in the last five years and losses have run into the millions of dollars. Insurance rates have gone up, and especially so for collectors who have sustained losses through thefts. The home is simply a poor place to keep coins.

Every imaginable ruse is used by the professional hijacker. He preys on both the large collectors and dealers, but not before he has established some form of entree that gives him at least a reasonable chance for a good haul. He becomes acquainted with collectors and dealers at coin shows, leads the intended victims on with promises of substantial deals or purchases at later dates, then ends up with a good outline for the theft. He usually is a stranger, but not always. He works calmly and convincingly.

Frequently the thief makes an appointment to show or look at coins, but always at the other fellow's address. His actions are about in line with the usual burglar.

Convincing telephone calls also are used ahead of visits to homes where valuable coins are kept. Of course, the caller is just passing through town and has only a short time to stay before going on to another destination. He could use a few rolls of 1950-D nickels and an uncirculated Indian Head cent set. Oddly enough these are exactly the coins the intended victim has for sale, and the hijacker learned the details a week before at a big coin show. Doubtless he has notes and plans relating to other thefts, but this particular one offers the best opportunity with a minimum risk.

On entering the collector's home the robber or robbers pull pistols, tie up the numismatist and his wife, ransack the house and finally leave with $10,000 worth of coins.

One bigtime coin thief followed a collector more than 500 miles before stealing a $25,000 collection of mixed coins from the trunk of a car. The hijacker became acquainted with the collector-dealer at a Gulf city coin show, had a pass key made while the victim's car was parked several days in the hotel garage, shadowed the car to another state, unlocked the trunk while the owner was eating breakfast, and took the big collection in less than three minutes. The owner took his eyes off the car only while he hastily glanced at the breakfast menu. The job was strictly a clever one all the way through.

The average coin thief would rather not have any form of confrontation in carrying out his robberies. He much prefers to rob your home while you are away from the house for a few hours, or preferably after establishing the fact that you are out of the city for a few days. This allows him to ransack the house in a more leisurely manner.

Half the fun connected with owning a large coin collection lies in the desire of the collector to look at it when the notion strikes him. He reasons to himself that it is a shame he cannot keep it around the house all the time. The bank box is entirely safe but it requires some trouble to visit the downtown establishment for the dozen reasons a collector may have. Finally he decides to keep at least a large part of the coins around the house for attribution, admiration, easy access, etc. This procedure may turn out to be a safe one, provided the collector keeps all details to himself.

Attractive display of coins is a large and vital part of numismatics. There are many holders for the purpose, but thousands of collectors use custom-made display cases that give the items and sets extra appeal.

The discussion of display appears in the chapter on theft only because it directly ties in with the opening it affords thieves who follow tempting possibilities. Around coin shows and association meetings we see elaborate displays that are competing for ribbons. Even a casual glance reveals the great value of the coin and paper money shown, a fact that should encourage the owners to inform all questioners that the displays are kept in safe places — not in the various homes.

Most of the coin shows are held on weekends, thus lending some weakness to the dealer's and collector's position where coins are on display. Schemers have been known to follow dealers to their places of business after coin shows for the purpose of robbing them during the transfer of the coin from cars to store vaults.

Frankly, the most dangerous aspects of display practices have been cited, in an effort to warn collectors and dealers of the chances of loss from theft. It is not all bad, and reasonable care in handling coins usually gets them around safely.

Coin dealers have tried to protect themselves with elaborate burglar alarm systems, and they have succeeded in stopping various attempts by robbers. However, they have by no means eliminated hijackings by thugs who were gambling for big stakes. Those in upstairs office buildings have been vulnerable to attack, since the element of surprise by sudden entry through the front door has been rather effective.

Small safes have been deterrents, but not always effective. Where two or three men work together, they may haul away safes weighing up to 500 pounds. Some thieves employ small trucks when posing as deliverymen, trash collectors or fruit peddlers to gain entrance, while alleys are the favorite routes of escape.

One large and trusting collector kept all of his coins at home. His house became a favorite meeting place for fellow numismatists. While away from the city on a short vacation he was robbed of all his coins. As evidence that the thief was a person who had been in the house before, hardly a thing in the home had been disturbed. Even a secret panel had been removed and replaced, while a small safe in the attic was taken.

Heavy losses by museums and historical societies have been staggering, among them the Yale University Museum and large Florida displays. Entry in some cases has been by extremely difficult routes, such as air vents and paths cut by welding torches.

Unfortunately the desire to display coins prominently by the true numismatist and the intention of the thief to take what he can get are in direct conflict. The situation is far from insurmountable but it requires a good sense of balance and precaution. Even heavy safes in homes are not the answer for many reasons. The following are a few good rules to follow:

1. Keep valuable coins in a bank box.
2. Don't take all coins out of box at once.
3. Never admit suspicious strangers to your home.
4. Give out limited information on the value of your collection.
5. Avoid unnecessary displays at coin conventions.
6. Learn to use bank rooms for trading purposes.
7. Keep an inventory of all coins.
8. Refer often to your bank box as home for your coins.
9. Carry adequate insurance on your coins, and especially so if they are to be kept outside a bank on various occasions.

Very small collections hardly justify special insurance of any kind, but where a value greater than $500 to $1,000 is involved it would be wise to make safety a paramount issue.

# CHAPTER TWELVE

# When
# Is a Collector
# a Dealer?

*String of 18 Lincoln Cents Overlapping*

The legal status of a coin collector is not a complicated one and varies largely with his activities. The Internal Revenue Service has been rather generous with the hobbyist who buys, sells and trades in limited way, since profits and losses roughly offset each other over a long period. Other tax sources also have recognized the hobby as an endeavor not designed primarily to increase capital without a corresponding outlay.

Hundreds of collectors have drifted into dealership through the side or back door, all the while wondering how it came about. The thin dividing line between hobby and business need not baffle the numismatist who goes about his normal pursuits in a casual manner, except in the case of suddenly expanded operations that may grow out of all proportion.

The expense of holding coins as a collection for 14 years roughly doubles their original cost, where interest on a comparable investment is considered. This means that a collection apparently sold at a handsome paper profit may not give the seller a genuine profit under any reasonable analysis that considers interest lost in its true perspective.

During one year a confirmed numismatist may attend the national A.N.A. convention, drive 2,000 miles to regional coin shows, maintain costly insurance and spend up to $1,000 in various ways. He usually makes no claims for deductions and considers his activities tied strictly to a hobby that provides both profits and losses through normal transactions. Even the valuable time used is not taken into account.

Obviously the net result of profits and losses cannot be considered a one-way street, in that any declared profit by the IRS should be offset by expenses incurred in the involved sales. When such expenses are included the collector often comes out with a net loss, not a profit. But substantial profits are possible where coins are purchased prior to realization that they are much rarer than suspected, then favorably liquidated.

There are certain important exceptions where profits should be considered in tax returns. Should a collector decide to join a promotional group and increase his activities beyond all reasonable casual levels, he may find himself in a business rather than a hobby. And should he make a large and rather rapid quick profit from a dealer-type promotion, the hobbyist turned promoter and plunger may do well to keep good records. Offsetting losses during the same taxable period naturally apply against profits, and so do any expenses incurred. At the end of the year our expanded operator may prove to be only the collector he was at the beginning, with losses and expenses wiping out the earlier profits from a few grand adventures. It is much better to stay in the non-professional ranks than to be carried away by a few successful deals.

So long as a collector remains a true hobbyist he appears to maintain his strict status quo position taxwise. This also applies to state sales taxes, where one collector sells to another on a casual basis requiring no such taxes. But coin dealers must collect sales taxes in a normal manner when selling various items to ordinary collectors. Courts have ruled that coins worth more than face value raise themselves from the class of ordinary specie and are subject to state sales taxes. In an Ohio suit a dealer held that the sale of U. S. coins at high premium values did not remove them from the ordinary specie classification, and that state sales taxes did not apply. The Ohio Supreme Court ruled that rare coins were similar to antiques and other valuable properties, and were taxable because they were no longer ordinary specie. Most of the states already had recognized premium coins as taxable items, where they were sold over the counter by recognized dealers.

The dividing line between hobbyist and dealer should not be difficult to define, yet it is determined by the nature of annual and year-to-year operations. A great deal of latitude seems to be riding with the ordinary collector who buys and sells at random and doubtless gives little attention to profit or loss. Certainly the individual who works regularly at a full-time job, yet manages to spend a great deal of time with coins on a pleasurable basis, is in no danger from the Internal Revenue Service.

The person who advertises regularly to buy and sell coins as an indicated dealer, frequents bourses as a steady merchant, maintains some semblance of a store in his home or principal place of business, joins with dealers in promotions designed to exploit certain issues, and buys all supplies at wholesale is flirting closely with dealership.

Conversely the collector who gives no thought to the hobby as a prime means of revenue, buys and sells on a random basis, ordinarily pays retail prices for supplies, and asks no special favors from dealers belongs so conspicuously to the amateur class that tax payments plainly are not applicable except in the case of local sales taxes.

Coin estates do not differ radically from other extensive holdings left to heirs under normal conditions, except that the question of face value versus market value may be a source of contention. Declaration should be within reason, but an attempt to place full catalog value on coins usually is out of the question. Common coins generally sell considerably below catalog values, and their advertised or recognized worth may be much less. More will be said later on the status of estates and mature holdings.

Requests from readers usually ask for information on the status of day-to-day coin transactions, rather than on the state, county, city and inheritance taxes that probably don't apply to small collections. A few think they should keep records of all trades, purchases and sales but many do not seem to know that a trade may not be a transaction final enough to draw net balances. The average buying and selling of coins among ordinary collectors is so near a break-even basis that records hardly seem necessary from a hobby standpoint. However, notes and records from a purely informational standpoint may prove useful.

The collector who sells a coin collection and immediately reinvests in items of true numismatic value appears to be in a safe position, and especially so where no attempt is made to reinvest in ordinary money with no premium value. The latter practice is a pure subterfuge but it might be difficult to prove that the newly acquired coins or currency did not have a special potential for future enhancement. Where the hobby angle seems to predominate, legitimate reinvestment after a sale appears a safe procedure.

The capital gain provision could possibly apply to large collections sold at substantial profits, and particularly so where they were bought as a strict speculation for quick gain. However, such transactions largely involve recognized dealers.

Many collectors use bourse tables as outlets for coins at small local shows, by displaying their collections as if they were dealers. It is believed that this practice does not represent a violation of any law if it is used sparingly and not as steady competition with regular dealers. Such collectors do not have state tax privileges and their operations might be compared with garage sales, etc.

Tax consultants mostly advise collectors to stay strictly in the amateur ranks. This may be done by buying, selling and trading within reason through the use of such methods as will not compete with recognized dealers. The impulsive trading of one coin for another at a coin club meeting, sale of a few coins through advertising, use of a stall or table at a small Saturday bourse, or purchase of a small collection from a stranger only represent various phases of the hobby at its best. Even a newsboy on the street is a dealer of a sort.

Most of the dealers of today started as collectors. A few of our current largest coin merchants became dealers almost overnight through the purchase of prosperous stores that were for sale for one reason or another. Such new owners necessarily passed through a kind of journeyman's period that exposed them to all kinds of deals they were unable to handle. One wealthy coin dealer who purchased a large coin store before he learned about numismatics bought almost everything offered at very high prices. The vanity of the man predominated until he was fortunate enough to obtain a partner who put the brakes on the wild spending spree. Which proves that only a skilled metal worker should buy a tin shop!

We should not regard the possible transition of a coin collector into a dealer as some type of disaster that may overtake all alike. "There comes the biggest hip pocket dealer in Texas," is the favorite greeting of a dealer in Dallas who guards his store with a jealous eye. Of course, he only half means it, yet he feels it smart to keep all of his big customers a bit off center with a taunting remark on the evils of private dealing of any kind. The bona fide dealer frequently holds a mild contempt for the part-time merchant who operates out of his home or his trailer.

A large coin periodical carries hundreds of advertisements of all sizes, yet it is impossible to separate all of the dealers from collectors who are dabbling around on a kind of "romancing streak". Most of the larger ads speak for themselves but the classified category seems to be dominated by the collectors. It might be well to brand the small advertisers properly, as "collector", "part-time dealer," "dealer", etc.

Since coin collecting is carried on as a hobby for fun and profit, let the various participants trade and traffic all they like. Admittedly much could be done to give the buyer more information on items offered, but presumably the publisher did the spade work before accepting the advertisement.

When is a collector a dealer? Again and again the question comes back into our lap. The whole matter is one of perspective and honest analysis. From coin club trading to selling a thousand proof sets, the participants seem to have their reasons for the various transactions. Petty swapping and sale of a large collection have their places in the hobby. Disposition of a ton of coins may not make the seller a dealer; and the buyer may be a simon-pure collector. Both the dealer and collector fit into the picture.

# CHAPTER THIRTEEN

# Developing a Balanced Collection

*1964 Bermuda Crown,
A Showy Coin*

"What do you collect?" is the standard question asked at all meetings. The replies obviously include the whole range of coins from circulated Lincoln cents to the very expensive early U. S. gold and silver. The odd, the old, medals, tokens, gold, silver and foreign items are favorites that somehow grew in the desires of millions of collectors and accumulators who manage to feel that certain coins have long since outgrown their ordinary specie designation. In short, something special has been found.

"How did you get started along that line?" is the usual question pressed by the person who plainly disagrees with the tastes of another. The tendency of certain collectors to stick with one issue perplexes the older numismatist who thinks he has learned that variety adds potential, profit and interest to the hobby.

Eventually advanced exposure will force most young collectors out of their shells, unless they choose to live in a limited, face-value existence. In such a case the neophytes were not inoculated properly to become enthusiastic coin collectors.

First efforts of the collector usually stem from a few lucky discoveries he has made under unusual conditions. Nearly all of the novices go off on tangents without guidance or serious planning. The average beginner pushes hard to equal or exceed his initial achievements, although some have been so nebulous and accidental that he will have difficulty in awakening to a reasonable course of action. Reference is made here to the thousands of beginners who have inherited valuable coins or found rarities in circulation through extended scanning operations. An old gold piece or an early large cent perhaps has been instrumental in shaping the collecting habits of a typical beginner.

Too much emphasis should not be placed on numismatics as a preconceived pastime. The chief objective should be to shoo collectors along a course that will not pass them by. A "balanced" collection to one person might be a form of monstrosity to another, but, one chief point involved is that of acquisition of many coins and issues that may not personally appeal to the collector. The veteran numismatist may have a distinct dislike for proof sets and the so-called "common" items, yet he goes along with them for many reasons. Many collectors remain blind to the various issues that may appear unpopular for the moment, or distinctly underpriced.

Recently a collector died and left a large estate in coins. Only a casual study of the estate inventory was needed to tell the young collector an important story. The deceased numismatist was a lover of all kinds of coins, yet he seemed to have had a strong preference for those scarce issues that were going begging on the open market. He had diversified to a wide degree, while admittedly holding rolls of coins he regarded as having had little numismatic value soon after their issue. Our late collector had also favored the obsolete and offbeat coins that were so slow in gaining recognition. Truly he had a balanced collection that could serve today as a model for any veteran. The estate was a very large one, and the coins were most prominent in their enhancement since original purchase. The inventory included items ranging from the commonest to real museum pieces.

Not all collectors are serious enough to give advanced thoughts to their inventories. Obviously they need help badly, but their greatest joy seems to lie in their own determination and self-reliance. Perhaps after a few bad mistakes they begin to seek advice and to reassess their position, but they remain a true cross-section of Americana.

The middle-of-the-road collector is the backbone of the hobby, in spite of all his faults. He buys a little of everything, breaks over occasionally and aquires expensive coins, diversifies on short notice and has the usual regrets at having missed certain juicy price advances. All of us would like to make him into the model collector at the drop of a hat, but unfortunately it takes thousands of these more or less disorganized souls to make the most interesting hobby in the world. The need for a truly balanced collection eventually dawns on perhaps half of all collectors, while the other half just rollicks along by acquiring such issues as will give them happiness for the moment. Which is to say that many collectors place pleasure far above profit.

Experienced collectors do not agree among themselves on the makeup of a balanced coin collection. Then is it any wonder that the novice should seem lost in the maze of available issues? Diversification could be substituted for balance in many cases, yet many of the wealthiest collectors have ridden the crest of a wave on such single issues as gold, silver dollars, ancient rarities and early American types. Specialization even extends to the dull issues of least popularity, but such collectors feel they have opened the door to ecstasy and future profit. Top quality in any selected group seems to be the goal of many collectors who disagree sharply on the word "balance."

Coin collectors who buy books and read them demand some specific type of information on the art of numismatics. They have wasted their time and money unless they have learned to open gates toward maximum exposure in all directions. This does not guarantee a plan leading to great wealth in a hurry, but it should place the collector in a position to participate in a full share of activity. Roughly half of all collectors are interested in coins as valuable items to be kept and enjoyed. The other half (largely hatched out since 1948) admittedly craves speculation and investment. The sentimentalist wants a sense of balance in his collection but it may be for display purposes only. The speculator may strive for that exact balance in his coins, but for another purpose.

One collector plans to spend $100 a year for coins; another has a budget of $1,000, while a third wishes to spend up to $12,000 annually to achieve a planned program. It may be seen quickly that the

96

rules for a balanced collection do not apply equally to these three collectors. The principal objectives here are to influence the $100 collector away from the temptation to buy so-called "junk;" the $1,000 collector away from the desire to plunge into one or two issues only; and the $12,000 collector away from speculation based on hearsay and casual advice.

Only a very thin line divides many of the chapters in this book. "Coins As an Investment", previously discussed in another chapter, ties in closely with efforts at achieving a balanced collection, the subject of this chapter. The rather long list of coins recommended in the investment chapter constitutes in a way a general balance that the average collector would wish to achieve. However, nearly half of all collectors insist that the investment and profit angles are not paramount in their activities, a fact that lends support to chapters on both investment and pleasurable aspects.

Recently a large, puritanical collector remarked that he bought coins without thought of profit. It was all a great fun game, he said, and there was no use to try to make money from it. In spite of his great, unselfish stand in the matter he appeared to be a very canny operator when approached as a prospective buyer or seller. It was later learned that this collector was a master at acquiring a wide spread of coins, all the while trading back and forth with unusual canniness. Something nice in every issue could be found in his bank box, although he claimed to embrace only the altruistic aspects of the hobby. Many collectors of this kind actually seem to believe their chief calling in the hobby lies in their unselfish ambition to help younger collectors, yet they know how to charge a pretty penny for their better material. However, in some cases the soft approach is a kind of mask to conceal a desire to trade or sell coins. This shrewd "merchandising" may be found frequently around coin clubs and non-profit meetings generally designed to expand interest in numismatics. There is nothing illegal about it, but a careful look usually reveals a well balanced and diversified position in the semi-dealers' portfolio.

Imbalance has spoiled many new collectors who came into the hobby with a desire to meet a limited or special condition. Such an impasse may stem from a desire for a long-term investment, quick profits or an urge from outside parties who have a selfish interest in the transaction. No greater disappointment exists than that following a poor acquisition that was doomed from the beginning. This placing of all eggs in one basket is typical of many beginners who overbuy through speculative influences.

Conversely a neophyte may be swept into a favorable position through a lucky or well-planned maneuver involving every ingredient of imbalance. A New York collector during the Depression invested $25,000 in uncirculated rolls of Lincoln cents dated from 1916 through 1934. They were a drug on the market at the time and the purchase price averaged less than two cents each. Many actually were scarce. All of the cents were sold about two years later at double their cost, but wait until you hear all of the story. The coins now would be worth several million dollars.

The collector certainly should not be so finicky about his inventory that he feels he should turn down any attractive purchase or sale. The main point to remember is that heavy stockpiling of one or two items may not be smart, even where a turn for the better is indicated. There may be some bad news to come later! A great deal also depends on whether the collector is a heavy trade or a long-term investor.

And so we see that a balanced collection to some is a matter of semantics, to others it means only wide diversification. The collector may look one way, the speculator another, yet a varied inventory can make both happy. Not all persons agree on the necessity for inclusion of certain groups in the bank box. But don't let fortune and pleasure pass you by. It is suggested that the reader review the tabulation in the chapter on "Coins As an Investment," then add such knick-knacks as will stimulate pleasure.

# CHAPTER FOURTEEN

*1964 Kennedy Half Dollar*

# Hoarding -
# a Matter
# of Connotation

*Hoard* (noun). An accumulation stored away for safeguarding.

*Hoard* (verb). To gather and store away or hide or future use, such as food, jewels and money. A wise, necessary or speculative practice to meet future needs.

Where does genuine coin collecting stop and hoarding begin? At what point does an individual cease to have the right to retire large quantities of current coins during a severe shortage? The Treasury Department in 1964 and most of 1965 was in a mood to get the answers to these questions, but fortunately for numismatics finally did not need to pursue the matter further after flooding the country with an adequate supply of all denominations except the half dollar. A showdown was narrowly missed, and thankfully so.

Use of strong talk, legislation with sharp teeth, and a warning to speculators were the principal weapons used to break the giant log jam that was keeping coins out of circulation prior to 1966. Actually and theoretically there is no law to prevent a citizen from putting aside coins of any kind that may be legally held as normal circulating mediums. This might exclude certain gold coins but certainly not the ordinary hoarding "stock" being hidden away by collectors and speculators during the current era.

It always has been the inherent right of a citizen to save for the future in any reasonable manner. It would be unthinkable to live under constant fear of confiscation of coin collections, formed by numismatists in the normal pursuit of their hobby. However, hoarding as a giant speculation against the common good in an emergency could result in stringent laws against the practice, and it is hoped this will not occur.

Nearly all metal money went into hoarding during the Civil War and it was necessary to replace it with "shin plasters", or small denomination paper money. Urgent pleas to restore the coins to circulation largely fell on deaf ears. Inflation was the driving force during those trying days that prompted retirement of hard money from trade channels.

Many conservative collectors purchased and put aside recently issued coins during the five-year period before 1966; somehow with the thought and hope they would steadily increase in value. Of course, they were hoarders in a sense that they were influenced by the hysteria then in evidence. Even such a plentiful coin as the 1959-D Lincoln cent was pushed to four times its face value in rolls, while the rush to obtain recent silver coins in quantity was almost embarrassing. Every current coin was in great demand.

The true collector and the speculator are two different people, yet their trails may cross on such a controversial subject as hoarding. Stacking away and mass purchases of recent coins are abhorrent to the veteran numismatist, but they seem to be great fun to the dashing accumulator who feels he has a promising commodity on his hands. Many of the most recent coins are available in 100-roll lots, yet they are regarded by the liberal collectors as true numismatic material of the future. And who knows for sure?

A long dissertation on what to keep versus what not to keep involves a great deal of border-line discussion that probably does not belong in any textbook. Since the legality of the question hardly seems involved, both collectors and speculators must choose their own courses. Technically, any considerable putting aside of coins is hoarding of a sort, but reason should be the guiding yardstick and economics an important consideration.

A half dozen fringe factors give the subject a great deal of latitude, and especially so during periods of shortage. Gold has been hoarded for 2,500 years by misers and fundamentalists, and even silver has been high on the list of the realist for a long time. The thinking of the great middle class has been affected by talk and hysteria to a point that it will go first one way then another, a fact that has accounted for many changes back and forth between hoarding and free circulation of coins. On the whole this great mass of bourgeois is both fickle and uninformed, at the moment not being favorable to stockpiling the most common of current coins. The author receives more requests on hoarding as a possible way "to educate our kids," etc., than on any single subject.

Where does the collector of the future fit into this scramble? At what point should he collect and hold coins on more than a normal basis? (In other words, hoard). Do such coins as most of those minted in 1955 have a real future when held in rolls? Will coin rolls eventually be broken down into singles at nice prices? Can a firm formula be developed to separate true collecting from hoarding? (The answer is no). Is hoarding an unpatriotic practice? Has hoarding proved profitable in the past? etc., etc.

There are two distinct types of hoarding (stacking away, if you don't like the frankness). One involves the holding only of coins that may be obtained at face value; the other, the putting away of the various issues of coins that already have attained a premium position. Some of the latter may be selling at two to 10 times face value.

The question of holding large quantities of coins immediately involves such big issues as the silver dollars, recent Lincoln cents, nickels and all common coins. The unfavorable factors are money rates at eight percent, lack of genuine rareness in the portfolio, changes in collecting habits, and non-productive nature of coins per se. Many of the medium large issues minted since 1945 are extensively held in uncirculated rolls, while others are genuinely scarce in uncirculated condition. The hoarder has a knack at running research on the coins he has in mind for speculation or investment, but his reasoning frequently is slanted toward the issues he already had in mind.

The opportunities that were open between 1920 and 1950 probably will not appear again. During that unusual period all hoarders who stayed with their holdings past 1950 profited handsomely from the subsequent enhancement. It was not unusual for a roll of uncirculated cents that was obtained at face value to be sold at $50. The

1931-S Lincoln cent was issued during the great depression and very few were saved in uncirculated condition. They were readily available at face value. If a "hoarder" had thoughtfully put away 100 rolls in 1931 at a cost of $50, he would now have rare coins worth about $200,000. On and on it is possible to point out even greater enhancement.

And we do know that if collectors had put aside a few rolls of the various early Buffalo nickels, all of us today would not need to pay so much for a single specimen. The hoarders really missed the boat from 1913 until 1931 by overlooking those nickels.

And so the question of hoarding, as opposed to holding out only a few coins, goes on and on. Perhaps the whole controversy is one of interpretation. We are literally suffering now from the *lack* of hoarding prior to 1930, with a distinct shortage of choice coins dated about 50 years ago. The tons of coins put away before 1966 still remain a questionable surplus, but the metallic content of many may take care of them even from a bulk standpoint. Inflation also has become a prime consideration.

Without doubt hoarding is the oldest of all practices designed to preserve life in a material manner. In Biblical times it was referred to as a form of necessary saving. During our own pioneer days hoarding was the setting aside of necessities for winter use and unforeseen contingencies of the early spring. The products might have been food, wood or money, but the stocks branded the hoarder as one who stored such expendable items as would be needed during periods of non-production. And, most of all, it was the hoarder who was able to sell from his stocks to the neighbors who had neglected to take necessary precautions along the same line.

Hoarding has taken on a more flexible meaning since the advent of the refrigerator, automobile and various modern facilities. Yet it retains both its legal and pleasurable aspects to many. The man who throws aside large quantities of commodities remains strictly within his rights, whether such items are hoarded for pleasure, necessity or profit. However, certain important exceptions may exist during war or national emergencies. Unreasonable hoarding may also correctly brand the offender as a miserly person who has developed an over-selfish desire to obtain a corner on a product to be held against the common good. The pros and cons of hoarding are so varied and marginal that in the final analysis the determining factors may be largely economical.

Thus we have seen hoarding run a long course from necessity to a form of rank speculation. It still retains many of its basis concepts, where the rainy-day aspects seem to call for frugality and the old desire to keep supplies on the shelf.

Nearly all of the old coin hoards were held as money in the bank, not as premium assets. Unfortunately there were not enough numismatists from 500 B.C. until 1930 to create a real sensation when a choice hoard came to light through death or accidental discovery. The big bucketful of coins simply went back into circulation from the estate as if they were of recent issue — as many were.

Since 1950 the discovery of a large hoard of choice old coins has caused a genuine stampede. An old miser in a large Texas city died suddenly about 1962 from malnutrition and self-neglect. He ran a small coin shop and was known to keep most of the items in two old safes. He was found dead on a dirty bed in a dingy back room. Rare U. S. and foreign gold coins were found on and under the mattress and all over the place. Value of the collection was close to a million dollars, yet the miserly old man drove a hard bargain with every transaction. He was one hoarder who finally hit the jackpot — in death.

Certainly not all hoarders are so gruesome and tight, yet liquidation of estates from time to time proves that the old collectors who saved or hoarded coins of low issue were on the smart side from the beginning. Rolls put away from 1930 until 1950 became very valuable with the big coin boom of the early 1960s. And they are still good. Putting away coins appears to be hoarding only when it is done in a big way.

An entirely new emphasis and interpretation were placed on coin hoarding, following the recent spurt in silver prices and the government's own retirement of silver coins from circulation. The general public, long ready to hide away silver coins on any signal from speculators, joined in the big run to put aside those 90 percent specimens minted before 1965. Countering this intention with its strongest weapon, the Treasury Department ruled that no silver coins of the

United States could be legally melted for conversion into speculative bullion. This immediately created a kind of impasse that made common silver coins technically worth only face value.

Recently a reader wrote and asked, "Tell me the real difference between hoarding and ordinary collecting of coins. One friend of mine has a large bank box full of recent rolls and proof sets. Another has about an equal value in scarce and rare items he regards as real numismatic items. Is one hoarding more than another?"

To attempt to answer this man's question would involve the reopening of about all we have said in this chapter. However, the two men described do represent opposite ends of the numismatic yardstick. One is at best an accumulator; the other at worst a collector. In the opinion of an old-school numismatist, the speculator with the following inventory would be a hoarder:

> 1,000 rolls of 1964-D cents
> 1,000 rolls of 1967 cents
> 1,000 rolls of 1967 dimes
> 1,000 rolls of 1967 quarters
> 1,000 rolls of 1967 half dollars
> 1,000 1961 proof sets
> 1,000 1962 proof sets
> 1,000 1963 proof sets
> 1,000 1964 proof sets
> $50,000 in face value of late 90 percent silver coins
> 500 $20 gold pieces
> 1,000 rolls of various dates of Kennedy half dollars

And so hoarding becomes largely a matter of connotation and purpose. Requests for information on coins with a future are numerous. Any form of putting aside involves a suggestion of hoarding, but perhaps not in the true manner. Metal, rarity and scarcity may be the driving forces back of the many accumulations of marginal nature. Only the future will show the wisdom of the young man who says, "I'll send my kids to college with profits from the sale of this so-and-so."

# CHAPTER FIFTEEN

# Speculative Buying Can Easily Backfire

*All Kinds of Coins Are Represented in Speculative Buying*

About half of the chapters in this book have touched on speculation as an attachment to the hobby in one way or another. This phase of coin collecting overlaps with investments, promotions and the general going along with rumors that tend to place certain issues in a position to move upward. Speculative buying may include the quiet accumulation of single, expensive items or the noisy acquisition of rolls, bulk material and key coins necessary to complete runs of dates and mint marks.

Much of the speculative buying is done in good faith, with the hoarders being at least courageous enough to acquire large quantities of the coins in question. On some occasions the promotional work is confined largely to whispers and rumors that so-and-so is a good buy and should advance rapidly. Not much money changes hands in such a situation until a favorable mood has been established for the issues under discussion. Actually the speculator who already has acquired a large number of certain coins is not above praising the investment qualities of his large stock! Frequently this is only a type of merchandising designed to permit the holder to pass his coins on to new owners at a good profit. Certainly the whole transaction is legal but it could be a case of *caveat emptor.*

Where a coin or group of coins is pushed on and on upward, the last man holding the items on the upswing is the victim of the spiral. This fact does not differ from speculation in any other marketplace, but it happens we are primarily interested in the gyrations of coins. Perhaps the dangers of loss through speculation are being exaggerated, yet the beginner should know that he is not likely to find a bird's nest on the ground.

Prior to 1940 speculation in coins was confined to the petty practices common to most hobbies. The big rush of new collectors after 1950 attracted much more capital, and soon the national meetings and bourses were buzzing with rumors of impending activity.

In spite of some questionable practices, the ensuing speculation had its good points. Many coins that had been dormant for 20 to 100 years almost suddenly found higher and more realistic levels. They were pushed upward because of rarity and the natural desire of so many new collectors to gain ownership. This type of promotion was needed to place scarce coins on a higher price level. And in most cases the genuinely rare coins managed to hold most of their gains established through a form of speculation.

At various national coin meetings from 1956 until 1965 blackboards were used by some dealers to keep the public advised on hourly Bid and Ask quotations on certain popular items like proof sets, silver dollars and the heavier gold pieces. Activity was rather frenzied and many prices today reflect the wisdom or fallacy of acquisitions dating back to those hectic years. Gold, rare coins, early proof sets and silver dollars are largely much higher than they were when prices were posted on those blackboards.

Coin trends are rather changeable and a bit fickle. This year it may be Lincoln cents; next year it may be Buffalo nickels or gold coins. Because of this possibility the collector should not speculate up what may be a blind street by going completely overboard on bulk material. Beginners are unwittingly affected by what they hear and read. The organized effort of a few speculators may change the collecting tastes of many who are groping only for enlightenment. Quality is the best buy, even from a speculative position.

Speculation, gullibility and a slight streak of larceny are so intertwined in many collectors that they overbuy items with low potential. It differs little from the old story of the tenderfoot or the journey-man who wants to take a short cut to profit after a doubtful initiation. Most of the larger speculative ventures find a willingness on the part of the eager buyers to take the trip. They have been over-sold on items that may appear all but hopeless to the experienced numismatist.

Perhaps a few specific cases of promotion and speculation in the past should be described to apprise the reader of certain conditions that have existed. A favorite promotion of the past was the frenzied action in certain rolls of U. S. issues. In some instances these rolls were sold on advice of the promoters, while in others they seemed to go right through the ceiling of their own accord. Such rolls as the 1950-D nickel and the 1955-D quarter were heavily promoted from time to time, yet their final, stable levels were still much higher than their prices at the beginning of their spirals. The 1950-D nickel was perhaps the classic example of all uncirculated rolls, in that many persons made fortunes on the coin while others lost on it. The price per roll of 40 advanced from $12 in 1955 to about $950 in 1964. The prices settled off to about $300 per roll in early 1973. Collectors who now hold this coin at a cost of $100 per roll feel themselves to be rather sharp operators, while those who got in very late at $900 per roll feel they waited a bit too late to get excited.

Speculating in coins in the 1950s was exactly like playing the stock market at the same time. Nearly all basic coins and stocks are much higher now than when they were being sought 12 years ago. Now we have problems with selectivity in both the stock and coin markets, still the same problems we have had all along. We have our Texacos and General Motors on the Big Board, and we have our $20 gold pieces and silver dollars in the coin field. However, most every collector would like to take a chance on finding a sleeper, even if in the name of pure speculation. Coin collecting has become a fast moving hobby that is not satisfied to accept a static situation where something may be hidden. Yet it is important to remain with basics, even in the height of speculation.

The word "balance", which we already have discussed, comes into the picture when investment is concerned, but it does not carry enough weight in the field of speculation. Promotional aspects usually carry us off on a single tangent, with the accompanying thought that it will be possible to "get out" on a rise before certain issues break. However, it is neither safe nor wise to condemn any phase of buying that has been highly successful in the past. Personally we may abhor many of the past practices that seem in conflict with a basic hobby, but at the moment they may prevail against what appears to be reasonable trends. Acceptance sometimes seems to come right out of the jungle.

Between 1948 and 1965 speculative buying probably was profitable nine times out of 10, provided the buyer was smart enough to take his profits. After 1965 the great upsurge was halted and the market for all coins became very selective. In 1963, probably the peak year for many issues, the scramble to get on almost any bandwagon prevailed. In late 1964 a hysteria of fear seemed to grasp the speculative influences, in that various sobering factors appeared to point toward the over-promotion of issues that were not scarce at all. In the ensuing adjustment many novices and plungers got hurt.

How do collectors get sucked into speculative spirals?

This occurs in many ways. The plunge may be petty or extensive and it frequently is done under the guise of investment. In fact, the dividing line between speculation and investment may be too thin to separate where the chief difference is largely a matter of interpretation. The beginner may start with $100 and the hope his eggs will hatch in one basket. The big plunger may follow either his own or a recommended plan of action to the amount of $20,000 or more. Money tied up in this manner may remain in the doldrums for a long time, with the speculator unable to decide whether he has a lemon or a bonanza.

Good examples of speculative influences were those responsible for spiraling such low-issue coins as the circulated 1924-D Lincoln cent, the 1932-S quarter and various Buffalo nickels. In 1964 it was difficult to weigh the merits of this little boom, and even today it is possible that such small issues as those mentioned will emerge as true investment items. The fact that the coins were promoted for about two years gave them rather high price plateaus that still belong to the future in many instances, yet various items may still be underpriced. Mention of specific coins under this example does not constitute an endorsement or indictment of the group.

For a few years after 1960 several "investment counsellors" advertised their services and promised practically every advantage but a firm guarantee that their recommended issues would return a profit. In some cases these services provided a type of brokerage acquisition for such groups of coins as were recommended for rapid enhacement. The customer agreed to purchase large lots of coins, with the understanding the seller was taking his "cut" or commission from the transaction. In one case the counsellor suggested the coins being bought should sell for 10 times their cost in 10 years, a rather fantastic claim for the wildest of speculators. His recommendations were based on the actual advances of certain spectacular issues to phenomenal levels. Fortunately the numismatic hobby frowned on this type of speculation to the extent that it hardly got off the ground.

The collector who blindly follows the advice of promoters may be buying what he wants as an ordinary hobbyist, not as a speculator. And if the collector is not in a hurry the joke may eventually be on the promoter. Conversely the wheeler-dealer may be acquiring the same material for a quick turn as a strict speculation. Thus time becomes an important consideration favoring one and perhaps upsetting the other.

"I enjoy speculating in coins but I always stay with those basic issues that seldom follow wide fluctuations. My favorite plan is to find coins on my own that seem to have been neglected; then buy and promote them myself. In doing so I try to stay with issues that will leave me a good "par" value in case of a bad selection."

The foregoing was the statement of a conservative speculator who in reality was an investor. He believed that any time a collector viewed coins from a bulk standpoint, such a person immediately joined the rank of the traders and dabblers, and he was the first to place himself in this category.

A large number of accumulators who were crowded out during the wild, speculative period between 1955 and 1965 are coming back into the field for another try at coins as an enjoyable diversion, not necessarily as a quick-profit experience. They learned much during their first tenure and now they think they can do better. This particularly applies to the new collectors who acquired chiefly recent uncirculated rolls and singles, and those who bought at the peak prices applicable to certain key coins after promotion.

Speculation is such a dirty word to many that they avoid use of it. Recently the author asked a dozen collectors to name a short list of coins now considered in the speculative class. The response was not surprising, except that it included several issues held in most investment portfolios. Here is part of the list:

1,000 tokens and old medals

200 pounds of the most recent foreign coins of various denominations

1,000 rolls of recent U. S. circulated coins

10 complete sets of U. S. commemorative half dollars

200 $20 gold pieces

$5,000 in face value of 90 percent silver coins

A large number of U. S. key coins now selling well below their former peak prices

Large quantities of common U. S. silver dollars

Large quantities of U. S. and foreign proof sets

Smaller quantities of any of the above for new collectors

Inclusion of a few of our most gilt edge issues in a speculative group was inevitable and understandable. In the case of the gold and silver coins, bullion prices are known to be highly speculative. Such fine stocks as Bethlehem Steel and a dozen others are selling so far below their former levels that they are considered speculative by many investors who own them. As stated earlier in this chapter, the line between the speculative and investment issues in coins is so thin that it may be nonexistent in spots.

The principal point we must learn is that speculation has helped to build this country, but it has also been called vision and looking to the future. In the field of numismatics the legitimate pushing upward of many dormant issues was speculation of a sort.

Yet the basic message we should put across is that no collector should speculate beyond his means. It may not be safe, and it is entirely possible to take hold of certain coins that already have had their big rise. It may also be well to remember that over half of all coin collectors follow the hobby for fun!

# CHAPTER SIXTEEN

*Shifting Image of*
*Lincoln on the Cent*

# Mint Errors,

# Misstrikes,

# Freaks,

# Oddities

While the various World mints are striving to issue perfect coins, certain collectors are searching for imperfect specimens that have somehow slipped by the inspectors and counters. Where one is trying to maintain a high standard, the other welcomes the mistakes as an addition to the long list of mint errors that is bound to accumulate over the years. Possibly no phase of numismatics is more interesting than that which centers around coins with all types of flaws. In the merchandising field such imperfect items would be classed as "seconds", but not in the realm of coins.

The degree of irregularity is the chief determining factor in the value of a misstruck coin. However, in their eagerness to classify slightly irregular specimens as acceptable items, many collectors may claim recognition for coins that show only slight flaws or variations from standard. A peculiar dot or slight date shift may be honored, but the real misstrike devotee wants unmistakable mint errors.

Thus proper classification and evaluation of overdates, freaks, die breaks misstrikes, mint errors, "fidos", and purely accidental oddities in coins has become increasingly difficult because of the anxiety of some to exploit minor variations that probably should go unnoticed. The desire is deep in every serious collector to find a new and over-looked variety or mint error that merits recognition, particularly in the early issues. But genuine discoveries come slowly with our current minting processes.

How much should an odd or unusual coin vary from the ordinary run to merit recognition as a misstrike or genuine accidental variety? Numismatists argue violently over this point and general agreement is out of the question. Freaks and imperfect coins are not unusual, but they should be recognized for what they really are. Stretching a point usually stems from pride in ownership and the desire to discover a distinct misstrike.

No two dies are exactly alike, and minor differences may be found in any series. A small blob on the nose, an imaginary pipe in the mouth or a slight die break may be interesting conjectures, but certainly they are only slight minting defects that were wholly unintended. Slight accidental variations generally are not recognized as worthwhile deviations from normal. In some of the older U.S. issues minted prior to 1815 it may be difficult to tell the accidental from the deliberate variation.

Although die breaks are not considered by many as true oddities, other collectors are inclined to include them as freaks or errors belonging to the misstrike family. Die breaks on a coin are fine metal seams or ridges caused by running of metal through die cracks. Die breaks may add distinction to an old coin, but one class of collector actually objects to such imperfections. Thousands of coins were struck after dies started breaking, and the imperfections should add distinction to such imperfect coins. Perhaps the common claim of many that ordinary scratches are die breaks has hurt the latter's cause. In the case of our large cents, determination of many varieties depends wholly on die breaks for their high values.

Basically there is a difference between the ordinary die break and the true mint error, but they will be discussed under a general section. Still the die error or imperfection has given us many interesting, recent mint oddities. All 1794 large cents were supposed to be essentially alike, yet at least 66 varieties are known. Variations were mostly negligible and actually went unnoticed at the time of mintage. A lot of small variations can be dug up if the researcher works hard enough.

Some misstrikes are so pronounced they have found their way into catalogs and coin collections everywhere. Dozens of minor errors are passed off as smaller mechanical oddities. Frequently efforts to force recognition of slight variations and errors are tinged with promotion and the collector will do well to remember this selfish practice.

Such slight mint errors as the 1922 "plain" Lincoln cent and the 1937-D 3-legged variety of Buffalo nickel had a difficult time in getting recognition as worthwhile mint errors. Lincoln cents were struck only at the Denver mint in 1922, yet we supposedly have with us a 1922 "plain" (no mint mark) cent of the same year. In almost every case the mint mark does show dimly, yet the cent is highly prized by many collectors. Supposedly the small "D" was obscured when the die filled. It is still a mystery to many collectors that such a coin can be accepted as a legitimate variation. The oddity was not even listed separately in catalogs for many years, but the very weak "D" finally won over the objection of the conservatives. This coin in uncirculated condition is considered a real rarity and is one of the most difficult to obtain in a choice set of Lincoln cents. Popularity of this cent doubtless has resulted in the filing off of the "D" on many 1922 Lincolns, but such an effort could be detected by close inspection. Thus we have seen that an oversight at the Denver mint has created a type of maverick in the error category. Acceptance by collectors and guide books eventually placed this accidental coin in the silk-stocking class, although the variation is admittedly slight.

The 1937-D 3-legged Buffalo nickel certainly had its troubles in winning official recognition as a freakish variety that shouldn't have appeared. It finally won listings in the various guide books and has become a rather expensive oddity among error enthusiasts. A die became clogged and the buffalo appears to have only three legs. Because of this striking oddity the coin is very popular with all collectors. Perhaps no other coin has been faked more than this one. The leg may be filed off rather cleverly, but fortunately there are a half dozen distinguishing markings on the genuine coin, other than the principal one involving the missing leg.

A classic recent example of a slight mint error is the 1955 double die Lincoln cent, a purely accidental variation that soon found its way into catalogs and public acceptance. This coin came about when the die jiggled or moved in some way during mintage. The obverse lettering showed a double impression that immediately caught the attention of error seekers, and the coin has become both popular and expensive. This oddity appeared in limited quantities, but enough to establish a kind of self authentication.

The heavy exploitation and almost immediate acceptance of the 1960 small date Lincoln cent reflect the hysteria that accompanied numismatics during the period from 1955 until 1965. The real reason for slightly enlarging the date after the initial 1960 coinage was not announced, but it is believed to have been done to strengthen the date area and to prevent clogging of the "O". The date enlargement was made at both mints. Such a limited date change would have gone unnoticed 40 years ago. The small date 1960 cents have achieved full acceptance in both regular and proof coinage.

Dozens of slight misstrikes and variations have been pushed for general recognition, but only a few achieved real stature. A large number of the so-called overdates and overmint marks probably are slight "happenings" in the usual striking. A small bit of metal on a date or mintmark certainly does not make a coin a true misstrike.

Oddly enough those coins that were misstruck in reasonable quantities generally turn out to be more valuable than the single specimen that merely "jumped a cog" or got caught in an off position in the striking process. Where a few hundred or thousands of irregular coins may be found to form an identical pattern, their genuineness can be easily established. A loner, or single misstrike, involves too much speculation to get the support it may deserve. Doubtless many altered or manufactured "mint errors" have appeared to hurt the chances of the single genuine oddity that may come along to pass into oblivion.

The common freak coins represent an intriguing group that stand out from perfect coins like a sore thumb. There can be no hairsplitting and arguing over such items. An entire collection of these oddities is both interesting and worthwhile. A case full of freak coins on display at a major show will perhaps attract more attention than a similar case filled with perfect strikes of all kinds. These radical misstrikes may be minted off center, doubly struck in some areas, damaged badly in striking, absolutely blank (unstruck) on one or both sides, or struck on wrong planchets.

By far the greatest number of freaks is caught at the mint, but a few do get out in one way or another. Around 1860 certain collectors reportedly had close connections at the mint, at least to the point they could obtain pattern coins and various favors. To what extent such favoritism affected restriking is not known, if to any extent. Freak coins actually were not popular in the 1860 period, and it is known that subsequently all U. S. mints have issued strict orders to employees to hold and account for freak coins.

Apparently a few 1943 Lincoln cents were struck erroneously or illegally in copper. All cents of that year were officially struck in steel and coated with zinc. Wild press reports have only increased interest in this misstrike, but in almost every case the cents in question turn out to be steel with copper plating privately applied. Use of a magnet tells instantly whether the principal metal is steel or copper. It is not known whether the very few 1943 copper cents were struck accidentally or by design.

Doubtless the most famous irregular coins of our period are the fantastic 1913 Liberty nickels, which in reality were a fraud so far as conventional issue was concerned. These coins are not true misstrikes, but could have been clandestinely struck at the mint to satisfy certain collectors. Officially there were no "V" nickels of that year, so the five that finally turned up, more or less in one group, must have been coined by design, not by accident. These oddities were perfectly struck and are not classed as freaks in any respect. They are classic examples of coins that have no legal right to fame, yet they have been fully accepted as extremely rare and valuable mavericks with tremendous prestige.

The first coins of the Greeks and Romans were mostly off center, irregular and even crudely struck prior to 100 B.C. Yet the collector passes over these faults gladly if the rare items are genuine. Such ancient coins were uniformly "rustic" but should not be classed as freaks or misstrikes from an average pattern. Slight variations

115

accompanied their acceptance at the time, and now, the obvious reason for this having been the ability of the ancients to throw out the real culls on a rather casual inspection. Certain issues of early Greek coins were out of round because strong emphasis was placed on weight and fineness, rather than on efforts to strike a perfectly round coin. The planchets were more or less "pinched off" and it is doubtful if the blank stocks were truly round in the beginning. The ancients took pride in their workmanship, with the early hand striking of the first issues having been rough enough to become outright attractive.

Freaks in the strict sense probably show up here oftener than they did with the ancients. This happens partly because of the much larger modern mintage, and partly through the automatic coining processes employed in United States mints. More freaks appear in the Lincoln cent series than in any other denomination but they occur in all of our issues.

A century ago a misstrike or freak coin simply was turned in at the bank or post-office by the holder, with the hope it would be accepted at face value. Possibly that was the most sensible thing to do, but now the eager collector pounces on any obvious irregularity as an important misstrike and simply makes the most of it as an oddity.

Many heated arguments rage over whether a freakish condition was caused by the striking or from plain kicking around under hard usage. The difference is important in the acceptance of an "ugly" coin that could have been run over by a train. At any rate the avid error seeker doesn't need much of an excuse to cull out and hold damaged or irregular coins showing strong question marks. They might be something special.

Freak and misstruck coins have proved a very good investment for collectors who have stayed with basic mint errors. The marginal items without pedigree should be avoided unless such additions are acquired largely on a protective basis. Possibly some may prove to be misstrikes, but the skilled collector soon learns the difference between a genuine mint error and a manufactured gimmick. But don't turn them in at the bank or post office because they happen to be struck badly off center!

116

# CHAPTER SEVENTEEN

*1796 Silver Half Dollar*

# Gold and Silver Coins Reflect Changing Times

*1901 Liberty Head Gold*

Gold and silver were among the earliest wealth and monetary standards of man. The Bible mentions both metals frequently, the first being in Genesis 2:11-12, with the two verses declaring that "the name of the first (river) is Pison . . . . which compasseth the whole land of Havilah, where there is gold; and the gold of that land is good." Again in Genesis 13:2 the Bible states that . . . "Abram was very rich in cattle, in silver and in gold." What an exciting start for two noble metals that are still around!

And so we see that gold has stirred the imagination of man since he learned in various ways to recover metals from the crust of the earth. The durability and beauty of the yellow metal contrasted with that of iron, a fact that attracted the attention of the ancients and caused them to accept it as a standard of value for all forms of bartering. They knew exactly how to value the gold in relation to sheep, cattle and land.

Early Persian, Chinese and Egyptian dynasties knew about and used both gold and silver as bullion and ornaments. The law of Menes, first of the Egyptian dynasties, declared in 3100 B.C. that gold would be worth 21/2 times as much as silver in commerce.

And so gold finally took its place at the head of the class because it had long been hoarded, pampered and even worshipped as a kind of sacred monetary unit. Other metals have been used more extensively in expendable forms, with countless tons of copper, nickel and even silver (since 1900) having gone into industry on an annual basis. But gold always has been chiefly used with an eye toward full recovery in the future, whether as jewelry or money. Only the gaudy use of gold in plating housetops and ancient bric-a-brac tended toward outright display of the metal in a more diffused form.

World production of gold since Columbus discovered America has been about 2,500,000,000 ounces, with an approximate current value of $312,500,000,000. When stacked as gold bricks it would make only a 50 foot cube. But if such a yellow shiny block could speak it could tell unbelievable stories of the romance, sweat, torture, greed and piracy involved in its production and transportation. Treachery and ambush were at one time almost as big a part in gold operations as the legitimate aspects of its movements.

Liberty is taken here for a slight departure from numismatics to give a short background of gold and its ability to hold a top position for at least 4,000 years.

Gold coins were first struck about 700 B.C., probably by the Lydians who had long used the metal in bullion form. The Greeks were quick to catch on and soon were striking beautiful gold coins with a rather crude process. By 330 B.C. the Grecian mints were able to coin gold pieces of great purity, although a little later (and also in the beginning) some of the gold coins contained from 15 to 50 percent silver in an apparent native state. Such debased coins were called electrums and there must have been a great deal of haggling over their lack of purity and desirability as a form of bullion.

Gold was an important coined money of the leading Asian dynasties from long before the birth of Christ until 1200 A.D. Rome was comparatively slow to push gold coinage but finally appreciated the importance of the metal. It is known that Greek gold coins were acceptable in Rome and other countries for a long time. Many beautiful gold coins were struck during the early Byzantine period, but debasement later became a problem.

Gold coins as a hoarding medium were generally popular from 700 B.C. until about 1835. After 1840 they became rather commonplace in the United States and circulated freely until 1933, except during such unusual periods as the Civil War. Perhaps the word "circulate" did not fully apply, but gold coins were readily available at any bank after 1870 for the asking. They circulated extensively on a mixed basis in the West until around 1880, after which silver coins attained a degree of preference.

In China and all of Asia gold, in one form or another, has remained the most accepted of all monetary issues. While such countries as Great Britain, France, Germany and the United States were passing through a rather placid gold period that lasted a century, the sheiks and rulers of Asia were grasping for all of the yellow metal they could get. A small premium on both open and clandestine shipments only made gold more popular from Saudi Arabia to India. Whether of English or United States origin, the sheiks, barons and rulers simply weighed out the coins as bullion and stored it in secret vaults.

A short review of World gold coinage may help the average collector make up his mind on the desirability of including the beautiful yellow discs in his inventory. Most collectors have regarded gold coins as too expensive to acquire on a steady basis, while others contended they really were the least expensive from an investment standpoint. The gold collector has felt safe in his own environment, knowing that the upward trend in metal prices finally has supported his basic position. The speculator for a time avoided gold in common dates because he saw the $20 gold piece linger awhile between $35 and $46. The enthusiastic gold buff has held all along that "some day gold will double and treble in price when we are looking out the window." Of course, no one could guess the future of gold as an investment item, except we did know that so long as it was the official exchange in our monetary system it did have some merit function to perform.

In the various boom areas, such as California after 1849, gold in any form opened every door. But it was inconvenient and inaccurate to handle as negotiable money when offered by strangers as having certain weight and fineness. Gold dust and questionable ingots were not always satisfactory mediums of exchange unless vouched for by some type of verification stamp.

Thus it was obvious that privately minted coins were a necessity in wild and hectic lands. Most of the private mints and assayers marked their coins and bars honestly, but some were short in both weight and fineness. Many of the large, more authentic gold pieces actually achieved semi-official status, and many numismatists now believe they should be considered special United States government coins.

Private gold coins were minted in North Carolina, Georgia, Colorado, Utah, Oregon, California and possibly other territories. They appeared in denominations of $1, $21/2, $5, $10, $20 and eventually the $50 issue. California was so short on small change that fractional gold coins in $1/4 and $1/2 denominations were minted in large quantities from 1852 through 1882. The miniature coins found ready acceptance in various channels.

The Mormons took a serious fling at gold coinage from 1849 until 1860 and struck a large number in several denominations. Most of these coins proved to be slightly underweight in comparison with our standard issues. Brigham Young was a leader in the movement for Mormon coinage, and even tried to achieve a form of nationalistic appearance in the job.

The United States minted gold coins more or less continuously from 1795 until 1933 in denominations of $1, $2.50, $3, $5, $10 and $20, and with various special issues struck as commemoratives. Our monetary standard was tied to gold through its bullion value, and even the spectacular calling in of gold coins in 1934 did not take us off the gold standard in the true sense of the word. The raise in the price of gold from $20.67 to $35 per ounce actually stimulated the yellow metal as a basic monetary unit. The paradoxical quirk only caused the whole world to seek and worship gold.

All leading World powers have minted gold coins, giving the collector a wide range for an attractive selection. Only one U.S. collector in about 10 starts in the gold category. Many wealthy collectors begin with gold coins almost exclusively, frequently from a prestige standpoint, and they remain the backbone of the yellow metal enthusiasts because of their spending tendencies and ability to remain solvent. "Gold coins are too rich for my blood", has been a favorite expression of the new collector, but if he had stopped to place gold in its true position he would not have been so positive in his belief that such expensive items could not be bought in even small numbers. Of course, the novice who confines himself to inexpensive current coins has not been interested in gold.

At one time the author received many requests from collectors and casual owners of gold coins, all asking about the legal status of ownership. A surprisingly large number of U. S. citizens still believe that gold coins may not be legally held in this country, while others hold to the old theory that the value of such coins must be held to $100. Gold regulations have changed several times since 1933 but under present laws any coin collector may acquire and hold all such gold coins as are available through normal numismatic channels. This simply means that all regular issue gold coins, U.S. and foreign, now held in the United States may be bought or sold without restraint, except a few minted after 1933. The former regulations held for some unexplained reason that gold coins minted after we supposedly went off the gold standard in 1934 could not be legally held. New provisions are more generous. Even this exception does not materially lower the large number of gold coins available as collectors' items.

Gold coins make good sense from any standpoint as a basis for a collection, and especially so for those who wish to place a part of their savings in numismatics. Use of gold for coins has declined to a negligible point, making obsolescence a strong factor in their increased popularity. An assorted collection of U.S. and foreign gold coins makes an attractive mixture of history, romance and beauty. Some numismatists want as much weight as possible with common dates, while others like the more colorful, expensive varieties. Any gold piece could tell an interesting story if only it could talk. From the discovery of America until past 1900 gold was sought fiercely in the New World. Spain became a great commercial power from the gold coins struck during 300 years, and many of those old coins are still available to the collector who can afford them.

A partial review of prices of the most common U.S. gold coins since 1933 reflects a steady rise of considerable proportions. Such coins as are shown in this table are those readily available at the present time and all may be legally held. Prices shown are for gold coins in Extremely Fine condition, or slightly better.

| | Denomination (Extremely Fine) | 1935 | 1945 | 1955 | 1965 | 1969 | 1974 |
|---|---|---|---|---|---|---|---|
| $1.00 | Type I | $2.25 | $5.00 | $8.50 | $25.00 | $40.00 | $100.00 |
| 1.00 | Type II | 2.50 | 8.00 | 12.50 | 150.00 | 175.00 | 475.00 |
| 1.00 | Type III | 2.50 | 5.00 | 8.50 | 27.50 | 50.00 | 100.00 |
| 2.50 | Liberty | 4.00 | 7.00 | 11.00 | 30.00 | 37.50 | 65.00 |
| 2.50 | Indian | 4.00 | 6.50 | 8.50 | 24.00 | 31.00 | 35.00 |
| 3.00 | | 6.00 | 15.00 | 25.00 | 160.00 | 210.00 | 325.00 |
| 5.00 | Liberty | 8.50 | 10.50 | 12.50 | 22.00 | 31.00 | 55.00 |
| 5.00 | Indian | 8.50 | 10.00 | 11.00 | 24.00 | 40.00 | 65.00 |
| 10.00 | Liberty | 17.50 | 20.00 | 22.00 | 27.50 | 38.00 | 80.00 |
| 10.00 | Indian | 17.50 | 20.00 | 22.00 | 32.50 | 50.00 | 120.00 |
| 20.00 | Both Types | 35.00 | 40.00 | 42.00 | 52.00 | 75.00 | 185.00 |

Rumors of higher bullion prices have persisted for 25 years, and gold coins have been affected frequently in relation to the intensity of the reports. Within each of the above 10-year periods, prices of gold coins jumped around nervously on price graphs, but after each decline the stabilizing prices were higher than those that prevailed before.

Gold coins are so tied to bullion prices that collectors may expect them to move up or down in line with the World bullion market. Any tendency of the major nations to throw gold overboard as a basic monetary metal would result in trouble for gold coins. However, no such movement is in sight and many experts feel that gold bullion prices will continue to rise. All we can say is that up to this time the demand for gold has increased while inflation has eaten away at the variables making up our principal expendable commodities. The recent spiral in gold coin prices was tied to rumors that bullion prices also would advance on a designated and official basis. The official U.S. gold price has been raised to $42.22 per ounce, but the so-called "free" or floating price has jumped to about $126 per ounce.

And so gold has been hoarded for nearly 4,000 years and collected numismatically for perhaps 200 years. About a century ago groups in Great Britain, France, Germany and the United States became attracted to gold coins as true collectors' items. They put aside known rarities, which could then be obtained at around 50 percent above bullion value, as a basis for solid collections with historical backgrounds. Occasionally one of these old caches comes to light to thrill the modern collectors who have stayed with gold coins as something to have and to hold. Royalty and industrial tycoons were among the first collectors to acquire gold coins as playthings of a sort.

The U.S. $1.00 gold piece was a controversial issue from the beginning in 1849 because of its small size and frequent loss from the pocket. Its diameter was increased in 1854, but it still had a way of finding all of the cracks and crevices. Coinage in the 1870s and 1880s was reduced to a pittance, partly to satisfy those who gave them as Christmas presents, etc. The president of an Eastern railroad reportedly took most of the annual coinage around 1880. The minting cost must have been very high where less than 5,000 gold dollars were coined during a single year. The dollar gold piece has increased rapidly in the collectors' favor since 1935. The millions turned in under the famous Roosevelt edict of early 1934 lend an air of sadness to all numismatists.

Silver coins have flirted around the fringes of the very select class since the beginning of coinage around 700 B.C., but it was not until 1964 that they broke from their moorings. Our admitted shortage of silver bullion, increased World demand for industrial purposes and the Kennedy half dollar combined to start rumors of an upward swing in basic silver prices. The United States Treasury held the price of silver to $1.2929 for a long time but finally turned the commodity loose to seek its own higher level. The accompanying publicity caused a run toward silver coins of all kinds, where they formerly were wanted chiefly for numismatic reasons. The result was their virtual disappearance from circulation during 1967 to become a bulk hoarding medium.

Rare silver coins have not been affected much in value by higher bullion prices alone, but the metal has gained prestige from its current shortage. Most of the World powers have discontinued coinage of silver in quantity, a fact that has upgraded the white metal. Silver coins of one country have become almost negotiable in another and the average collectors know this fact. They have become popular with the low-geared collector who has been tending more and more toward acquisition of large foreign silver coins.

Our own silver dollar is a classic example of a coin that has run the full gamut of both human and metallic emotions. First coined in limited quantities in 1794, the U.S. silver dollar was issued periodically through 1935. It became a popular coin in the West but was not accepted in quantity in the East and Middle West. Pork-barreled and pushed by Western interests, the silver dollar was minted in huge quantities from 1878 through 1935. Since they were largely stored in Treasury vaults for 60 to 80 years, their coinage seems to have been largely to satisfy the producers of Western silver.

It would be repetitious to describe again the huge dumping of

*Rare 1861 'O' Double Eagle ($20.00 Gold)*

*Rare 1872 "CC" Silver Dollar*

countless millions of silver dollars that began in 1962. They were offered to all takers at face value in $1,000 bags as a gesture not yet fully understood. At any rate only about three million of the silver dollars finally were left in Treasury vaults, and now every collector in the country is trying to get even one of the scarce "CC" cartwheels.

The silver dollar market has become a kind of dabbling ground for many collectors and speculators who are trying to outguess the market. The commonest circulated ones were selling at double face value or more early in 1969. Full sets of these dollars (all dates and mint marks that are available) have become very popular with conservative collectors, with the scarce and rare ones seeming to have gained much respect in numismatic circles. Some of the low yearly mint issues are very rare, and completion of a set involves a large outlay. All in all, the U.S. silver dollar is a rather respectable coin!

A short summation of the position of both gold and silver in numismatics reveals a greater place in the sun for both. Only some type of repudiation of one or both of the metals as basic monetary standards would serve to hurt their position. Certainly no such move appears in the offing. It would require a lot of undoing to destroy the love of gold and silver among those people who have buried and worshipped it for so many centuries.

Gold always has been a convenient metal for coinage, since it enabled a man to carry a small fortune in a sack. Times did change some in the nineteenth century, when gold became a form of commodity. Again a change came in the twentieth century, but in favor of gold as a precious metal to own and to hoard against adversity.

Silver coins have just tagged along, trying to maintain some semblance of a ratio to gold. But inflation and a threatened shortage of the white metal have given it a new value in numismatics. Both gold and silver coins have largely joined the obsolescent class, in this case to their advantage. Nobody can guarantee the continued upswing in demand for coins in these metals, but at the moment they are riding high. At least high enough to make most collectors wish they had joined the club earlier and in a bigger way.

# CHAPTER EIGHTEEN

# Tokens and Medals

*Tradesmans Tokens and Commemorative Medal*

Tokens and medals are regarded by many as fringe or peripheral forms of numismatics, to be taken or left at the collector's option. However, these important items should be considered a distinct addition to any collection because of their historical significance. The medal tells largely of achievement; the token may remind us of our hard times and shortcomings. The medal never was nogotiable as money, while the token frequently was.

The complete range of tokens includes every type of metal disc that served a hundred purposes. Some were issued by merchants to pass at full value at their stores; many were politically inspired as advertising mediums; others represented a pledge of some kind. Metal tokens played an important but unofficial part in our weak monetary efforts from 1790 until 1865. While strictly unauthorized by state or national governments, these little substitutes actually achieved a strong measure of acceptance and respectability when properly sponsored by organizations and individuals.

Strictly speaking a token is a symbol of good faith, a gesture of acknowledgment, a distinguishing mark, a pledge of some kind, or a printed or engraved object of metal or paper showing an obligation or purpose. It may have been a piece of metal for trading purposes with a designated face value, but most of the early tokens involved metal items depreciated in value from that which it replaced. Some were substitutes for real money and were issued on a "promise to pay" basis. They ran all the way from the most sarcastic political purpose to semi-medals honoring famous people or events.

The sutlers, and their various tokens, were indeed an interesting group of peddlers who followed an army, or lived in a garrison town or camp and sold provisions to the troops. He was primarily provisioner, a small vendor or trader recommended or licensed by the army as a kind of portable post exchange. The sutler was a friend-in-need during the long monotonous days in camp, but a soldier's nemesis on pay day. These peddlers were well known to our Revolutionary armies and continued their activities through the Civil War to a lesser extent. Their Civil War tokens were fairly numerous and interesting. They were struck in copper, brass, lead, nickel, tin, copper-nickel, hard rubber and zinc. Shakespeare, in "Henry V", referred to our peddler friends in this manner: "I shall Sutler be unto the camps and profits will accrue."

Although tokens were issued all over the world in one form or another, the U.S. collector today largely confines his acquisitions to the following:

Merchants tokens of 1789 to 1850 (U.S.).
Hard Times tokens of 1832 to 1844 (U.S.).
Civil War tokens of 1861 to 1864 (U.S.).
Canadian tokens of 1815 to 1870.
Merchants tokens of 1870 to 1930 (U.S.).
English tokens of 1650 to 1817.
Recent tokens (transportation, etc.) of 1890 to 1969 (U.S.).

The early merchants tokens were an unusual lot, in that some seemed to be struck as advertising pieces while others carried denominations and passed for money. The later ones apparently were handed out to remind the buyer where he could obtain the various wares of the day. They were issued prior to 1850 in about 20 states and territories, and many are available to collectors. Some are very rare in any condition.

The hard times tokens represented a stirring period of about 13 years, during which sarcasm, free speech and political conniving reached a new high. These tokens were about the size of our large cent and many were fairly well struck. Politicians were quick to take advantage of economic conditions by flooding the country with tokens designed to influence the voter. They were political medals of a cheap sort with patriotic motives, but these were quickly followed with the real hard times tokens having a wide variety of political and satirical declarations and designs. Sensing the use politicians were making of the copper discs, merchants were quick to take advantage of such a means of advertising. The burst of "store cards", as they were frequently called, lasted in intensity from about 1832 to 1844, then continued at a lesser pace until the introduction of the copper-nickel cent in 1857. These tokens are available to collectors and are not expensive.

Lack of a stable banking system in the United States undoubtedly was a factor in permitting the issuance of hard times tokens to get out of hand. One of the chief subjects carried on many of the tokens was related to the instability of private banks.

The acute shortage of coins from 1861 to 1864 prompted the issuance of millions of Civil War tokens. They were chiefly struck in copper, the size of the current Indian Head cent, but they are also found in brass, lead, zinc, tin, white metals and silver. Many were of patriotic design; others carried advertisements. They passed as money in many areas but were declared illegal as specie in 1964. Many of these tokens were well struck and now are popular with collectors. They are not expensive, but have endured their contempt as substitute money with remarkable tolerance and acceptance. Small hoards of these tokens are occasionally found in the East through excavations and various hiding places. Many carried the heads of Washington and Lincoln and they were issued in more than 20 states.

Canadian tokens were issued because of a lack of coins and possibly for advertising purposes. However, they lacked the satirical theme that our hard times tokens carried. Our neighbor to the north was passing through a transitional period, when various provinces were puzzled over a political course of action. Many of these tokens are available and they make a nice addition to any collection.

Merchants tokens of 1870 to about 1930 consisted largely of discs representing amounts the various stores would pay in trade for the tokens. During the period of use they might be held by plantation workers, lumber mill employees, share croppers and the like, but after return to the store and redemption they were considered worthless as collectors' items. However, many stores did keep an inventory of both outstanding and "on hand" trade tokens, as a form of cash in many cases and outstanding liabilities in others.

About 1962 an old merchandising firm in Oklahoma found thousands of its trade tokens case aside in a back room. Use of the tokens had long since been discontinued and they were known to be worthless. However, they had been used in territorial days and

were boldly marked "I.T.", for Indian Territory. Sensing a demand from coin collectors for the old tokens, the store owner placed them on the market and received more than five times face value for the sets containing the 5-cent, 10-cent, 25-cent, 50-cent and $1 tokens. Thousands of dollars in profit was made from the old tokens that already had been written off. Territorial items in any form are in great demand from collectors, in fact so much so that they have been counterfeited on many occasions.

In England after 1600, millions of tokens came into circulation only by sufferance and not by authority of the crown. The national coinage was so inadequate that all types of special tokens were minted privately to fill the need. Periodically the government was able to stop this illegal coinage, but it was not until 1818 that the various tokens were ordered withdrawn from circulation. A large variety of English tokens is available and they are not considered expensive. Most are well struck and attractive.

A large number of United States collectors favor recent tokens as inexpensive items. They may involve transportation, state sales tax, political subjects, fairs and gambling. Such material is of interest to the young collector who will graduate into higher numismatics as his budget and interest grow. Souvenir pieces from the various World's fairs of the past 80 years are popular and typical of those tokens now available.

Some tokens in the groups listed are very rare and expensive; others are common. Of the Civil War tokens and cards, there are more than 9,000 varieties known. It is hard to believe that one of the cheaper ones will sell for more than a dollar if in nice condition, while a really scarce one will command many times as much.

Medals largely stem from achievement. The Greeks were among the first to award medals, primarily to winners of athletic events and later to persons in other fields of excellence. The Romans started just before the birth of Christ with a long series of medals honoring its emperors and perhaps some of their favorites around the court. Much later nearly all ruling dignitaries were influencing the casting of medals as a form of self-glorification and declaration of power. William the Conqueror (r. 1066-1087) is believed to have been the first English king to receive an official medal as head of state, but his successors seemed to have caught on with little outside help. Actually an authorized medal was not out of line for kings and queens, even if they fell into the bad habit of awarding medals to their court favorites and cronies who were expected to respond in case of trouble. A medal was a medal, for all of its virtues or faults, and soon some of the finest specimens started finding their way into collectors' hands at very high prices.

The medal tempo stepped up fast after 1400 and gradually it became the symbol of great honor for the recipient. For a long, long time a medal was a one-of-a-kind gift, but gradually similar medals, in limited numbers, were presented to heroes and patriots for deeds jointly performed. This increased the outstanding number to a point that permitted many of the recipients to sell their gold medals (on the sly) for their bullion content. Some of the medals struck by European rulers from 1600 to 1900 were rather ornate and very well designed. Collectors paid big prices for those that were well authenticated.

The United States government has been a generous striker of medals of various kinds. The Presidential series in bronze run from Washington to Nixon and the complete set makes a magnificent addition to any collection. They are not expensive. Any collector may get a list of available medals by writing the Superintendent of the Mint at Philadelphia. The medals come in various sizes, and honor heroes, events, cities, states and achievements.

The first real test of a medal's value lies in its sponsorship and justification. Was it officially authorized by a government, society for historical and patriotic achievements or a national meeting of some kind? Was it a purely local issue designed to have limited or souvenir appeal? Was it conceived as a private promotion based largely on a profit motive? Did issuance of the medal simply ride the skirts of a great tragedy or achievement? Many foundations of honorable intention have struck medals, but the motivation was not lofty enough to make them valuable in the eyes of collectors.

Recently private corporations were formed to issue medals honoring famous people, tragedies, states and various causes. Although they have no official sponsorship that is authorized by a government, many of these medals are very well struck in metals ranging from platinum to bronze. Some stem from club-like arrangements, while others may be acquired by the public without membership. A few of the larger clubs require purchase of a series of medals at fixed prices, with those in the better metals being limited in number as a possible protection against over-issuance.

Only the future will determine the numismatic value of privately struck medals of this kind. Some may achieve real rarity as time goes on, while others with large issues and mediocre designs may eventually be regarded as souvenir pieces of a sort. Many medal collectors are acquiring the better issues of this kind, with the thought and hope they will grow in popularity. In all candor, the young collector should attempt to cull out such private medals as may be rushed on the market as pocket pieces or obvious souvenirs, unless he feels the reasonable prices may justify the largest possible variety as mere show pieces. By 2050 many of the medals now being offered privately may be extremely valuable, but that is a long time to wait. In all fairness it should be explained that the avid collector acquires medals for pleasure and variety, without regard to their value next year or the next. Perhaps too much emphasis has been placed on enhancement as a reason for joining the medal ranks.

Other available medals for collectors include a wide variety from old military decorations to political streamers of a sort. Germany and France issued thousands of decorations that could be classified as medals, and some have become popular with U.S. collectors.

Some of the most ardent numismatists spend all their spare time in antique and coin shops while visiting in distant cities, with the hope they will pick up unusual or valuable medals. Others make the rounds at coin shows for the same purpose.

And so the collector of today may have some difficulty in determining whether the item he is about to acquire is a medallion, medal, token, decoration or souvenir piece. This confusion only adds to the interest of the vast group. The range extends from a choice gold medal struck in honor of a European ruler to a souvenir piece of a World's Fair. The price may be $500 or $1 but a collector somewhere will take it. The medal somehow smacks of achievement and glory, whether of the 1775 or 1969 vintage.

# CHAPTER NINETEEN

# Rolls and Bags
# As Bulk Ventures

*A Bag of 1968-S Lincoln Cents*

The temptation to collect and hold coins by the roll and bag has been most pronounced since 1940. Closing of the San Francisco mint in 1955 touched off a hoarding spree that absorbed most of that institution's coinage during its farewell operating period. The denouement was so publicized that California banks and speculators generally were able to control distribution of the greater part of that mint's output — 44,610,000 cents and 18,510,000 dimes. No other denominations were issued during the closing year. And to this day those "S" mint cents and dimes are held chiefly in rolls and bags, thus defying all efforts to place them in general circulation. If a comparatively large issue of cents and dimes from San Francisco could be held in quantities and run skyward in prices, why not get on the bandwagon, the onlookers asked, and do a little speculating in rolls and bags in a general way?

Coming at a time when new speculators and collectors were entering the field from every direction, the roll-and-bag interests subsequently sought to acquire large quantities of *all* current and recent coins that appeared to offer *any* enhancement possibilities. This activity soon resulted in such a large inventory of common coins that a great dumping process occurred during and after

1964 by the collectors and speculators who had thought for a few years they could do nothing wrong. Many of the coins had been acquired at or near face value, but the shrinking process took away much of the profits.

The 1964 decline occurred chiefly because of the race of almost everybody to lay aside any coins that were inexpensive. Even the 1959-D cent, a very common coin of large issue, had been pushed upward in rolls of 50 from face value at any bank to nearly $2.00 during 1962 and 1963. Such rolls as the better Roosevelt dimes and Jefferson nickels more than trebled in value between 1958 and 1964, with most of the other denominations moving sharply upward. Almost everybody seemed to want coins in quantity.

The opening paragraphs of this chapter certainly are not intended as an indictment against the roll and bag buyer. When pursued on a sensible basis quantity acquisition of coins can make very good sense for many reasons. The point in question is simply that whole-sale indulgence in speculation, as related to acquisition of ordinary coins on a spiraling market, may not prove profitable in the end. Obviously selectivity should be an important factor where the buyer has price enhancement in mind.

We may scold the dedicated or casual collector who insists he is putting away a few rolls or bags of coins "for his grandkids." Of course, if every collector followed such a plan there could even be a shortage of all kinds. But rest assured, the average collector doesn't want to invest heavily enough in the current clad coinage to do any harm. Most of the doting fathers and grandfathers are going back a few years to select rolls that already have shown some promise, and they may prove to be smart for their thought-fulness. We may have more than 20 million coin collectors in another 20 years.

The simon-pure collector has long looked on coins in rolls and bags with a form of contempt. He asks how it is possible for any numismatist to break away from the single coin to dabble in quan-tities of issues that are plainly plentiful. Our conservative friend may break over occasionally to buy a duplicate coin, but he remains ever the straight-laced bird. Actually he chooses to remain on the prissy side of the question.

The roll and bag operator has a ready answer for the criticism coming his way by saying simply, "Wake up; times have changed. Millions of new collectors have come into the picture. A roll of coins now hardly equals the single coin of 1936. The recent spurt in silver prices proves that rolls and bags of a few years ago have been profitable."

Admittedly a bag of coins is a pretty big chunk of "numismatics". A roll seems more tolerable to the average collector. The bulk activity was born of past scarcity of the old issues, speculation and the hope future values will soar. The big void now in the issues coined between 1900 and 1940 may have given some false hopes to the current speculator.

A very few of the cautious and fussy collecctors of 1921 and 1931 casually obtained a small scattering of rolls of uncirculated coins of those years and wondered whether they should be extravagant. The thought of putting aside a bag of cents ($50), nickels ($200), dimes ($500), quarters ($1,000) or halves ($1,000) never entered their minds. Some of the yearly issues did seem a bit shorter than usual, but whoever heard of tying up money in sacks of coins!

It may seem like daydreaming, but let us suppose a collector had been smart enough to put aside a bag of all denominations and mints of 1921 and 1931 at face value. He would be pretty old now, but let us further suppose he is still living and has all of the bags of those two years. Here is how his estate would look, coinwise, of course:

| Bags of Coins | Face Value | 1974 Value |
|---|---|---|
| 1921-P Cents . . . . . . . . . . . | $50.00 | $ 90,000.00 |
| 1921-D Cents . . . . . . . . . . . None Minted | | — — — — |
| 1921-S Cents . . . . . . . . . . . | 50.00 | 600,000.00 |
| 1931-P Cents . . . . . . . . . . . | 50.00 | 40,000.00 |
| 1931-D Cents . . . . . . . . . . | 50.00 | 180,000.00 |
| 1931-S Cents . . . . . . . . . . . | 50.00 | 170,000.00 |
| 1921-P Nickels . . . . . . . . . . | 200.00 | 200,000.00 |
| 1921-D Nickels . . . . . . . . . . None Minted | | — — — — |
| 1921-S Nickels . . . . . . . . . . | 200.00 | 1,000,000.00 |

135          *(Continued on next page)*

| | | |
|---|---|---|
| 1931-P Nickels | None Minted | — — — — — |
| 1931-D Nickels | None Minted | — — — — — |
| 1931-S Nickels | 200.00 | 200,000.00 |
| 1921-P Dimes | 500.00 | 3,750,000.00 |
| 1921-D Dimes | 500.00 | 3,500,000.00 |
| 1921-S Dimes | None Minted | — — — — — |
| 1931-P Dimes | 500.00 | 150,000.00 |
| 1931-D Dimes | 500.00 | 225,000.00 |
| 1931-S Dimes | 500.00 | 225,000.00 |
| 1921-P Quarters | 1,000.00 | 775,000.00 |
| 1921-D Quarters | None Minted | — — — — — |
| 1921-S Quarters | None Minted | — — — — — |
| 1931-P Quarters | None Minted | — — — — — |
| 1931-D Quarters | None Minted | — — — — — |
| 1931-S Quarters | None Minted | — — — — — |
| 1921-P Half Dollars | 1,000.00 | 1,600,000.00 |
| 1921-D Half Dollars | 1,000.00 | 2,400,000.00 |
| 1921-S Half Dollars | 1,000.00 | 6,000,000.00 |
| 1931-P Half Dollars | None Minted | — — — — — |
| 1931-D Half Dollars | None Minted | — — — — — |
| 1931-S Half Dollars | None Minted | — — — — — |
| TOTALS | $7,350.00 | $21,105,000.00 |

The above totals are all the more phenomenal because there was no coinage of quarters and half dollars during both years. Present prices of the 1921 and 1931 issues indicate two principal facts. There were few collectors, and the active numismatists of that period were not interested in putting aside uncirculated coins.

The largest coin dealer in the Chicago area decided on three occasions to stop dealing in rolls in the mid-1940s and early 1950s. Following each complete liquidation of his roll stocks he was forced to get back into the roll business, both at public demand and at much higher prices. Unfortunately he was trying to eliminate his roll department at the most opportune time for acquisition. The dealer liked to sell single rarities, and regarded rolls as the backwash of numismatics. He proved to be wrong and later admitted he should have remained with the trend toward an expanded roll market. All of which proves that dealers often make the biggest mistakes. Coins held in rolls may be grouped in a general fashion for the benefit of the collector who has not yet ventured toward the bulk market. In each group there are a few exceptions, such as the 1950-D nickel, 1955-D quarter and certain Roosevelt dimes. A rather loose listing follows for the flexible-minded collector and accumulator:

1. Uncirculated after 1964 (very low or no premium).
2. Uncirculated from 1940 to 1965 (low to medium premium).
3. Uncirculated from 1940 to 1965 (medium to high premium).
4. Uncirculated from 1880 to 1940 (medium to high premium).
5. Uncirculated from 1880 to 1940 (very high premium).
6. Circulated from 1940 to 1965 (very low to no premium).
7. Circulated from 1940 to 1965 (low to medium premium).
8. Circulated from 1880 to 1940 (low to medium premium).
9. Circulated from 1880 to 1940 (medium to very high premium).

Various additional listings could be made but the above should suffice for the average purpose. The most common of the circulated coins after 1940 actually carry no recognized premium, but when offered in full rolls some of the "S" and "D" coins may bring nominal premiums. The knack and effort going with assembling a whole roll of a certain date may have their rewards in the form of a sale at a profit. The roll market between collectors is considerably higher than between dealers.

The roll and bag market in any coin comes about when scarcity or low coinage is suspected. It has not been unusual to run the price of uncirculated cents or nickels to double face value or higher with rumors they are going to be scarce. Cases in point are the 1968-S cents and nickels. These coins have sold at much more than face value since the first part of 1968 and doubtless premiums will be paid for them from here on out. Naturally they are heavily held in rolls and bags. The public have been able to absorb large issues of coins on the strength of rumors. The 1964 Kennedy half dollar is an outstanding example of a coin that could not be put into general circulation.

In 1939 an unbiased collector in Houston was putting away one roll each of all uncirculated U.S. coins. He advised new collectors to do the same, with the assurance that some of the issues would prove valuable. His chief goal was to make a return of five percent on the money invested in rolls. His collection was much later sold at auction and brought a fabulous sum. Some of his roll sets for certain years brought 20 times their original cost. At the moment current rolls of clad coins certainly do not seem to hold such a future as our 1939 friend had, but perhaps many of the older rolls now available have distinct enhancement possibilities.

Coin rolls have become a form of commodity, to be held intact and bought or sold as a unit. Nobody seems to want to spread them out as singles unless a real shortage develops. Occasionally a conservative numismatist will say, "Look, this roll of dimes will give 50 collectors one coin each. They can't be very scarce when they are available by the roll."

Many roll enthusiasts believe that holding coins off the market as singles will boost prices if there is an increased demand from new collectors of the future. The roll hoarder is a patient person and many are still hoping to take care of their grandkids with the final residue. The real point seems to be simply this: Would the available rolls, if broken down, undersupply or oversupply the regular collector?

Both rolls and $1,000 bags of silver dollars are readily available on the open coin market. The Treasury Department must have issued close to 200,000 bags of silver dollars during a short period after 1960, and at face value. These coins have proved a good investment because of higher silver prices and increased public interest.

All 90 percent silver coins are being held extensively in roll and bag lots. Since removal of the former melting ban, these bulk coins have taken on a new interest and value. Silver bars made from 90 percent silver coins obviously are not as desirable as those containing "pure" silver for commercial purposes, but through re-refining they may be changed into bars capable of acceptance in any channels. Removal of the melting ban definitely improved the position of the 90 percent silver coins as a commodity, not as a controlled piece of money.

Large numbers of Kennedy half dollars are being held in bags, particularly those of 1964. This coin has quite a bit going for it, but the 433 million coinage appears too high for any runaway race on the up side. Perhaps no other coin is so widely held. Ask any neighbor or friend if you would know who has a dozen or so thrown to one side. Kennedy half dollars dated after 1964 are only 40 percent silver, and at the moment it looks almost silly to hitch your wagon to such a coin. It is not wise to condemn a 40 percent silver coin, or any coin for that matter, yet the flood of Kennedy half dollars after 1964 has gone into hiding as if they were something really rare.

Buying rolls and bags now is very much like shopping around for a good stock or bond. Rolls may be found, dated after 1935, that look attractive. Then there are the silver dollars; the really scarce circulated items that sell well as single coins; low-priced commemoratives; circulated type coins after 1840, and the rather expensive key coins of the circulated 1909-S cent and 1932-D quarter varieties. To prove a good investment rolls should increase in price by at least six percent annually. There are always many fluctuations but the basic curve must be upward to justify holding coins in quantities.

# CHAPTER TWENTY

# The Millionaire Coin Collector

*U.S. Indian Head Gold*

The wealthy collector represents several distinct types of individuals in the numismatic field. Obviously he is an ordinary human being, just like the rest, and he enters the activity with all the fears, enthusiasm, wonderment and misgivings of the rank novice. The seven principal types found in the big money ranks follow:

1. The true numismatist who tries hard to build a rare and balanced collection through reasonable purchases.
2. The plunger who buys at top prices nearly all choice or designated coins offered — at least for a while. He usually gets over this tendency.
3. The rather tight, miserly business man who drives a very hard bargain to prove he is no easy mark. He may sometimes work through an agent.
4. The rank speculator who frequently goes along as a partner with skilled interests that look for "sleepers" in the bulk or rarity field.
5. The "accidental" collector who becomes interested in coins through an inheritance, bank contacts, friends or a shrewd purchase of a hoard.
6. The business tycoon whose confidence has been gained by a coin dealer.
7. The "moonlighter" who holds down an important job, yet finds time to deal heavily in coins. He could be considered a mainstay in numismatics.

Around any coin convention the wealthy collector is a conspicuous figure. He accounts for a large percentage of total business, always going from table to table for a special purpose. One year he will be looking for rolls, the next year for gold or rarities. The principal trends may be set by his actions, but his hunches may be no better than those of the lesser collector. Dealers watch for the big buyers with mixed emotions, because some are looking for bargains, others are willing to pay fair prices for anything they need. But all are held in respect because of their buying power.

Recently an industrialist commissioned a prominent dealer to acquire the principal rarities, with no special regard for cost. The multi-millionaire wanted a collection that would include every coin of every type available in the better groups. Some of the coins sought might be unique (only one known), while others would be in the ultra-select class. The collection finally was put together at a cost of about five million dollars, after which the owner died. The collection was given to the Smithsonian Institution in return for a special tax deduction for the estate, a procedure that attracted national attention towards numismatics as a glamorous hobby for the rich and poor.

Heavy buyers of proof sets, gold, commemoratives and rolls may eventually have a pronounced effect on the market for such items. The smaller collectors have many times been benefitted by increased activity they were unaware of. Conversely a big selling movement may have the opposite effect. However, on the whole the wealthy collector has greatly increased the magnitude of the hobby with his volume operations.

Following World War II and prior to 1964 a great gold-buying spree took place in this country. Import regulations were eased for a few years, soon after it was learned that a tremendous amount of U.S. gold coins were hoarded and for sale in Switzerland. The $20, $10, and $5 pieces were brought in on an ordinary import license basis in unbelievably large numbers, and conspicuous amomg the buyers were the wealthy collectors. These coins are still mostly held here and make up a large part of our gold coin inventory.

Of course, there was nothing illegal in acquisition of the coins, but our unfavorable trade balance finally caused the Treasury

Department to shut off the normal and somewhat casual importation of gold coins from Switzerland and France. At the time of purchase between 1946 and 1964 common gold coins actually were on the speculative side, because of the cost of holding them from year to year and the considerable premium on them above face value. The big buyers finally lucked out through an improved demand for the yellow metal. At least the heavy importation around 1960 gave us a good stock of the large denomination gold pieces that otherwise would be resting in Switzerland and France.

Obviously the pronounced gold importers were not numismatists of the old school, but they were showing the way in a new direction. They made up an enlarged segment of the hobby, that of the investor and the speculator. Whether we like it or not coin collecting has become a pastime for both profit and enjoyment. It has many avenues for activity.

The small collector was able to ride the coattails of the big gold buyer and obtain the coins he wanted at the time. Perhaps we are putting too much stress on the wealthy collector as a controlling factor in numismatics. He makes the same mistakes the novice makes, except that he makes them in a bigger way. He spends more money than the neophyte but he has no more fun. His activities may run the prices of certain issues upward for a time but they may decline after he has ceased his buying spree. He may acquire only extreme rarities, but the poor collector's worn 1914-D Lincoln cent may carry just as much meaning.

Many famous men became coin collectors in a normal manner. Some of those well-known hobbyists of the past were King Victor Emmanuel II, King Farouk I of Egypt, Adolph Menjou, Hollywood, and Josiah H. Lilly, Indianapolis, Indiana. Farouk went for both quantity and quality. Victor Emmanuel tended toward World coins of all denominations, with rarities included where necessary. Menjou was both an advanced collector and accumulator of the more common issues. Lilly put together a fabulous collection of rarities that eventually went to the Smithsonian Institution after his death via the tax deduction route. The Farouk and Menjou collections were sold at auction, and hundreds of collectors were able to obtain coins from these groups.

Occasionally an industrialist will become infatuated with coins as a hobby for a few years, only to lose interest for some reason. Such a collector really gives the hobby a whirl before deciding to give it up. This type of man usually is the impetuous kind and is well known for jumping around with his pursuits. Such large collections are disposed of through auctions, public and private sales.

Many of the largest collectors are distinct boosters of numismatics and friends to the beginners. They attend coin club meetings in the role of lecturers and discuss trends that are so important to the novices. However, some of the collectors with the highest financial ratings do not ever warm up to the hobby in a big way. They may be conscious of their lack of knowledge, or perhaps they look at a dollar pretty hard before spending it.

The desire of wealthy men to own rarities has pushed the price of these items upward to a great height. In such coins as early U.S. gold, silver and copper pieces, many have been priced out of reach of the modest collector. In all fairness, however, it should be added that the average collector never sought such coins anyway, a fact that clears the big buyer from any conniving or collusion.

The thinking of the modest and wealthy collectors are not so different after all. The smaller one may be buffeted a bit by the waves of the larger one, but he may also be helped by the upward market action caused by the activities of the giants. It is somewhat like the big real estate operator who buys land all around the small landowner. The man with the small parcel may be helped by the transaction. And he wasn't able to purchase the big block in the first place. So there must be room for all kinds of collectors.

# CHAPTER TWENTY-ONE
# Paper Money & Numismatics

*Republic of*
*Texas Currency*

Although the dictionary and various encyclopedias do not include paper money as a part of numismatics, currency has become so much a part of coin collecting that it might as well be recognized as a part of the whole plan. No special exception is made for or against paper money in coin stores, conventions, coin journals and coin clubs, a fact that merely places currency of all kinds in the same hobby category as coins.

"Do you collect paper money?" is a question heard almost as often as queries about gold, silver or foreign coins. Around conventions and club meetings currency may run the various coin issues a close race in popularity and volume and business. A national association for the benefit of paper money collectors is maintained, and some of the wealthiest men in the country follow the hobby with advanced interest.

A surprisingly large number of modest collectors keep a careful watch on paper money reaching their wallets, the beginning that usually leads to a more professional approach. Catalogs and standard guides showing the scarce and rare issues are available, and the younger collectors scan their pocket money with the hope of finding a real rarity.

The old "saddle blanket" type of currency was discontinued in 1929 in favor of the small size paper money we now have. The searcher of today hardly expects to find one of those old quilts in circulation, but he is constantly on the lookout for one or more through other sources. The novice who has read thrilling stories of the discovery of valuable paper money in circulation, in hoards and at tellers' windows is just as curious as the dedicated coin collector who keeps looking for his first 1909-SVDB Lincoln cent.

Press reports of the appearance of large amounts of the old-style currency in estates frequently cause a stampede of collectors toward the scene. And some of the old bills turn out to be rare and very valuable. Bankers were favorite collectors of old currency, due to their desire to put together different series of national bank notes. Next in line was perhaps the plain hoarder who put aside any bills he could spare. A few years back an old woman who distrusted banks was found to have hundreds of old bills hidden away in mattresses, books and various closets. Some were scarce and valuable. European hoards have been found on occasion but they are rather uncommon. The chances of finding a big bundle of valuable currency are so remote, however, that it might be better to purchase what is needed than to entertain any wild dreams!

The recent silver certificate boom probably attracted more public attention to paper money than any other development in the hobby. It was truly a bonanza, a bird's nest on the ground, an unexpected windfall and a great game for bargain hunters. Who ever heard of Santa Claus? How could any type of money redemption be so profitable?

The Treasury Department decided to redeem outstanding silver certificates in silver granules or bars, on the basis of $1.2929 per ounce. At about the same time the fixed selling price of silver was withdrawn by the Treasury and World prices shot upward. In effect the government was selling silver at $1.2929 per ounce on a firm basis to silver certificate holders, while the open market was much higher. In one year, from June 1967, to June 1968, millions of silver certificates were turned in for redemption at a substantial profit to holders. Silver received for this currency obviously was worth much more on the open market than the fixed price charged for it in the redemption process, having made it possible to sell the silver at an immediate profit.

Bank tellers and cashiers, speculators and the general public joined in the big redemption process, an exciting procedure that attracted thousands of persons toward currency collecting as a hobby. It might be well to mention that the common, circulated silver certificates not turned in for redemption immediately became a piece of paper worth exactly a dollar in ordinary Federal Reserve notes or current coins. The author has received at least a thousand requests for information on the future of such silver certificates at premium items. The answer is simply that the dirty, "raggy" specimens now hanging around don't look promising. Perhaps they should have been turned in. Still they may be in big demand in a hundred years or so. Who knows for sure?

The paper money enthusiast should first arm himself with at least two catalogs or guides. Collectors of currency have increased by 300 percent in the past 10 years, possibly more. From our earliest colonial efforts through the current series, paper money — some good and some bad — has had its struggle to gain the soundness required for acceptance. Only a strong and reliable government can issue currency of enduring value. It was not until 1861 that the United States finally developed an acceptable paper money provision that was foolproof in its intent and planning. Some of our early struggles toward sufficiency will be discussed in this chapter.

The remarkable fact that this country groped along for more than 75 years in an effort to meet its public obligations, while trying through questionable methods to provide sound paper money for commerce, reflects inability to develop a monetary plan of full national scope and adequacy.

Our first major bank act in 1791 set up a nationwide banking structure, operated principally by private interests authorized to issue paper money that could be used for tax payments so long as it was redeemable on demand in coin. The new law obviously let down the bars to all types of private banks that issued currency with little regard to assets backing it, and failures during panic periods prior to 1861 were numerous. Depositors could not understand the questionable explanations offered by bank officials after the money was lost. The early private banks were opened under a kind of "states rights" arrangement but had the semi-official nod of the national government. Many of the banks were well managed and solvent, however.

The paper money collector has a colorful range of currency from which to choose. Most of the older U.S. issues have become rather expensive but the new collector will find a large number of recent types at modest prices. The currency purchaser of 1955 now has a handsome profit all through his collection. The fact that the supply of large-size paper money issued prior to 1930 has been inadequate to meet collector demand, has brought prominence to all of the older notes. The novice frequently starts with the worn (circulated) bills, then graduates to such choice currency as he can afford. The following general grouping covers the principal paper money issues of this country:

1. Colonial currency
2. Continental currency
3. State bank notes
4. United States government issues
   a. Demand notes (payable on demand)
   b. Legal Tender (United States notes)
   c. Interest bearing notes (various)
   d. Silver certificates
   e. Coin notes
   f. National bank notes
   g. Fractional currency (shin plasters)
   h. Gold certificates
   i. Federal Reserve bank notes
   j. Federal Reserve notes

Refunding certificates were issued in 1879 but they are considered by many as a kind of bond. These certificates are excessively rare in the first of two types. Some privilege and latitude is taken in arranging the above grouping.

Excellent paper money catalogs and library material have appeared since 1950 and the new collector need not wonder about most of his currency items. Beginning with our struggle with England it is possible to trace development of paper money to a sound medium of exchange. For 75 years after 1785 coins were used chiefly in the average hand-to-hand transaction, but the exchange of valuable property necessitated paper obligations. It was eventually inevitable that a real national currency backed by something tangible or designated would be used.

The Civil War created the great and almost instant call for paper notes that specifically promised the holder something in return for the piece of paper he carried in his pocket. The real moment of disaster forced our government to recognize that the backing of all money was a national, not a state responsibility, a condition that came about in 1861 and remained with us.

The American colonies actually issued paper money and notes of a sort, largely as necessity caused by a coin shortage and the need for larger exchanges of money. Such colonial notes were payable in Spanish milled dollars, gold, silver or some type of guaranteed acceptance without protest. It was difficult at any time to determine the real backing of these old notes, and redemption in many cases was doubtful. Much of the colonial currency probably was issued as a form of script that hopefully would pass for money without question. So long as no one refused it, circulation was uneventful.

Another tragic adventure in early paper experiments was the issuance of Continental currency to meet the cost of the Revolutionary War. Doubtfully conceived and inadequately backed, the issue had only limited support in any circle. Eventually those caught with it last were the losers. This paper money was issued from 1775 until 1779.

The bank act of 1791 obviously let down the bars to all types of private banks. These state-licensed banks issued colorful currency but its beauty certainly was no guarantee of solvency. Bank officials frequently speculated with deposits, and when it was impossible to pay off they simply announced that their investments had turned out poorly. The brazenness with which many wildcat banks shrugged off their insolvency was appalling. Depositors generally were forced to accept what they were offered on liquidation. So many of the state-chartered banks went broke that the currency now remaining in collectors' hands is usually called "broken bank notes," certainly not a very fitting reminder of a long but weak banking period in this country.

Not all of these state-chartered banks operated inefficiently. Many were controlled by honorable families and stockholders that prospered and remained in financial fields after the Civil War. The series of panics between 1810 and 1860 were instrumental in the closing of many banks that were overextended.

These so-called "broken bank notes" still are plentiful and inexpensive, giving the modest collector an opportunity to acquire a colorful assortment at low cost.

The country's grand venture into fractional currency from 1862 to 1876 proved successful, and all items now known are recognized as collectors' items. These miniature notes were issued in denominations of 3, 5, 10, 15, 25 and 50 cents and served principally as small change during a stirring period. Known as "shin plasters", these small notes were attractively printed in many types and sizes. Some limitations on payment were prescribed, but all such notes were real money, at least up to certain amounts.

Collectors usually concentrate on U.S. issues put out from 1861 until the present time, giving them a wide range of choices and prices from which to choose. Condition is just as important with currency as with coins. It is not within the province of this chapter to list all of the exciting currency items available from the U.S. series, but the coin collector who has shunned paper money up to now will do well to venture into the vast and intriguing realm of currency. The finest engravers in the world create the designs for our paper money and some of the past issues rank with the most beautiful in the world. From the intense green to the gold coloring of the past, our notes are unexcelled.

Confederate and Texas currencies are extensively collected in many parts of the country. While not as well executed in design as the U.S. series, many of these notes are remarkably striking in appearance. The first Confederate notes of 1861 show a peculiar quality that appears to depict great determination through tranquility and a desire for justice. The last issue of 1864 is inferior in quality to earlier issues.

Republic of Texas currency is interesting and rather inexpensive. It should be a part of every paper money collection, since it represents a stirring transitional period.

For the collector who likes paper money in general for its beauty and historical significance, he has little trouble in finding both. For the collector who wonders whether paper money has been a good investment, let him compare present prices with those of 1955. For the non-collector of paper money, now is a good time to start.

# CHAPTER TWENTY-TWO

# Foreign Coins Have Wide Appeal

*Maria Theresa Thaler, Obverse*

The field of foreign coins is almost limitless and the price range will fit any pocketbook. The collector's greatest problem will be his difficulty in covering all of the interesting fields offered. Starting with the ancient Grecian, Roman and Egyptian series and continuing until the latest issues of today, the numismatist may follow World history as it unfolded through its coinage. Truly a great cruise into the past is open to the adventurer who acquires and evaluates the hard money of other lands. Battles for freedom, economic superiority and a better way of life are reflected by many of the issues coming from countries much older than the United States.

The rise and fall of great nations, vanity of their rulers, overthrowing of despots, the constant struggle of young republics, and the desire for pursuit of happiness may be discerned in the transitional and fringe periods incidental to national adjustment. Coins tell a continuing, even if subdued story of a nation's greatness or mediocrity. And so from Alexander the Great to Nero, to Isabella I, to the Napoleons, to Kaiser Wilhelm, to Elizabeth II, we find no special modesty among the rulers. They all wanted to be pictured on coins of their ruling periods, supposedly as a medium of love and public relations but frequently as a show of strength, rightful inheritance and vanity. Many of their mottoes indicated special appointment from God, not from and by the people.

The young, emerging nations made possible since World War II have been issuing beautiful and exciting coinage, not with an act of defiance but from a desire to express the humility and freedom of the people. Most of these coins are inexpensive, except in the case of proofs and certain commemoratives, and they offer the collector an opportunity to get in on the ground floor with issues reflecting the history he viewed in the making. Liberty has been the constant theme carried by coins of new republics for 200 years, with the United States, France and Mexico prominent in this category.

Any plan for collecting foreign coins must be geared to expenditures and time allotted. The modest collector will need to stay with the inexpensive issues or limited items in the better groups, while the advanced numismatist may wish to touch on a wide range of issues from ancient to latest modern. A general grouping follows:

Early ancient (600 B.C. to 100 B.C.)
Later ancient (100 B.C. to 500 A.D.)
Medieval (500 to 1500)
Early modern (1500 to 1700)
Middle modern (1700 to 1800)
Later modern (1800 to date)

The foreign coin collector is lost without adequate literature. Authentication and accurate classification are half the pleasure in the hobby. "That must be a Russian coin of some kind", is the typical expression of the casual accumulator who guesses at what he has. "I know this old silver piece is rare but I am not sure whether it is of German or Austrian origin," is another common conjecture. Both standard and auction catalogs may be used to advantage in any type of identification, while books applicable to the various countries usually add color and romance to the bare facts the collector may already have. After a long and hard look it is a big thrill to find an illustration and description of the coin under scrutiny.

Ancient coins have been touched on lightly in the various chapters. They are available in copper, silver and gold and represent one of the least expensive links with the deep past. The price range for ancient coins in the various metals runs from perhaps $1.00 to

$1,000. The badly worn bronzes serve as a starter for many beginners, with the better and older gold pieces preferred by the wealthier numismatists. Counterfeits in the silver and gold issues are known, and some are better struck than the originals. Even experienced dealers have been fooled by some of the better copies.

The ancients were great coin hoarders, with earthen jars having been a favorite container in the burying process. Occasionally large jars of very old coins are found while using modern machinery for the usual digging operations — foundations, excavations, pipe lines, etc. This type of discovery alone has been a prominent factor in keeping ancient coin prices within the reach of the average collector. However, all choice specimens are from two to four times higher now than in 1955. The modern surge in collecting interest has been further stimulated by publication in English of many fine books on ancient coins.

The best way to start an ancient coin collection is through a reliable dealer who will help with the early groundwork. Another approach is through the aid of an experienced collector who is unselfish with his advice. This phase of the hobby seems to have been neglected in the past. Now is a good time to explore its wonderful possibilities.

Every imaginable type of specialization will be found in the ranks of foreign coin collectors. A survey reflected numerous approaches to this branch of numismatics, some well organized and others rather haphazard. Most of the collectors contacted admitted starting with little or no objective. A few of the plans follow, aside from the ancients:

> One to three coins of the various countries
> One country only, as complete as possible
> Emphasis on ethnic considerations
> Topical coins
> Bronze or copper coins
> Silver coins
> Gold coins
> Coins of a continent
> Proofs
> Crown (dollar) size silver coins

Odd money
World tokens
Recent proof and commemorative sets
Coins showing certain famous people
Coins of a certain period

The young foreign coin collectors of 20 years ago principally started by searching through great quantities of coins offered for sale by dealers. It was one of those "anything in this box for a nickel" deals that appealed to the young bargain hunters. Nearly all of those novices have advanced to a better type of collecting, as evidenced by the millions of dollars spent annually by our foreign coin collectors.

Coins of Canada and Mexico are far up on the popularity scale and there are large numbers of collectors who favor the issues of these two neighbors. A better study a few years back of the coins of Mexico established many rarities that previously had not been regarded as even scarce. Canadian coins rank among the most beautiful in the world, while the early issues of Mexico reflect that country's noble struggle for liberty.

A collection of silver crowns makes a showy, historical display that is hard to surpass in the numismatic field. These beautiful pieces date back to about 1500 and most of the principal countries have issued coins in this size at one time or another. Our own silver dollars, along with those of Canada, are classed as crowns in World parlance. The forerunner of our silver dollar was the Bohemian taler, as it was indeed the prototype of all talers, dollars and dollar-size silver coins, in at least a general way. The first dated issues of the Bohemian talers were coined in 1518. Many of the subsequent crowns of other nations had all the beauty of medals and they offer an unexcelled cruise into numismatic lore.

Two outstanding crowns that became World or regional standards in their time were the Maria Theresa taler and the Spanish milled dollar (eight reales or pieces of eight). Passing in commercial channels everywhere on a bullion basis, these two famous coins were the acceptable mediums of exchange that forced other countries to attempt to match them in various ways. Our first silver dollar of 1795 was conceived as a means of giving the United States a large coin competitive with the Spanish milled dollar.

The Maria Theresa silver taler was of Austrian origin and has served as standard currency in much of the Arab world for nearly 200 years. Always dated 1780 and carrying the beautiful silver appearance, the coin has made good sense to traders who felt secure at least to the extent of its bullion value. Of course, those now available are of recent coinage but they are accurate copies of the originals. Natives of parts of the Near East and Africa did not like paper money and they soon learned to recognize the Maria Theresa taler on sight. Russia is reportedly counterfeiting this coin to finance many of its ventures into the Middle East, using a lower silver content to make it really profitable. The Maria Theresa taler has long been a favorite with collectors and is inexpensive.

The Spanish milled dollar, or pieces of eight, was a real international workhorse from about 1730 until almost 1850, and it was not until 1857 that the United States officially disclaimed it as a legal tender equivalent. This coin was frequently cut into halves, quarters and eighths for use as change, the practice having given rise to the expressions, "bits", "two bits", "four bits" and "six bits." All foreign coin collectors will want to include this colorful silver crown among their conversation pieces.

The quality of minting processes may be traced from century to century through an examination of coins. The hand-struck specimens from Greece and Rome were rough in their own way, yet they reflect a certain beauty because of it. Many of the early coins were out of round, struck badly off center and lightly imprinted, yet they should be valued for these slight imperfections. Introduction of improved steam minting processes about 1836 lent uniformity to coins, with better centering and lettering. Each large nation has carried on a rivalry stemming from the desire to issue the most beautiful coins. European countries have achieved a medal-like appearance in some of their outstanding issues, with some of the silver crowns of a century ago reflecting a high type of engraving. However, some of the most recent limited foreign coin types seem to have striven more toward ornateness than practicality. It is known that some of the rulers of two and three centuries ago were displeased with their images on coins. One good example *should* have been Charles III of

Spain. Surely his nose was not as ugly as shown!

For those who want specialization in World coinage, make the necessary study and take off. The field of numismatics has greatly increased in such countries as Great Britain, France, Italy and Spain. The United States collector will find assistance in the groundwork accomplished since 1955 by foreign collectors. Conversely the foreign numismatists have borrowed much from United States collectors, even in the limits of their own fields. Researchers in New York, Chicago, Washington and other American cities have worked extensively to study and classify coins of other countries, with emphasis on those of Mexico, Canada and the ancients. The joint effort has aroused a new interest in World coinage among collectors in our own country.

A recent and somewhat glamorous development in foreign issues includes proof sets and special groupings designed to attract collectors in this country. Panama, Canada, Israel, South Africa, France, the Bahamas and many small countries have since 1950 issued various sets for sale at rather high prices. In most cases the output is limited to tempt the numismatist who insists on some type of exclusiveness. Australia also ventured into the special set category, but offered such packets to all comers for a time. Israel has used special coin issues as a substantial revenue project. It is difficult to evaluate special sets as true numismatic material but they add considerable color to many otherwise drab issues.

Speculation has not been so pronounced as in the United States issues, yet the better foreign coins are much higher than they were in 1955 or 1960. Some of the Mexican, Canadian and English issues have been spiraled by manipulation, a fact that should be remembered by the bulk collector of foreign coins.

Gold and silver coins have become scarce in all foreign countries. Silver recently passed out of general circulation in Europe in less than a month, following our own redemption of silver certificates and the jump in bullion prices. The older silver coins — crowns, etc. — also advanced to new price levels. The solid collector who started with foreign coins 15 years ago is now sitting in a comfortable seat. The haphazard collector of today should revise his thinking and start on a well-charted course to enjoyment.

# CHAPTER TWENTY-THREE

# Selling a Coin Collection

*Trading Is Popular
in Many Quarters*

At some time during the span of a collector's activity it may become necessary or profitable to dispose of his coins. Hopefully it is while the collector is living and in good health, but it may not be. Principal reasons for selling large collections are:

1. Voluntary dispostion
    a. Switch to another phase
    b. Loss of interest
2. Financial difficulties
    a. Individual
    b. Dealer
3. Liquidation of estates
    a. Haphazard mixture
    b. Volume hoarder
    c. Deceased numismatist

Most of the experienced collectors know the various selling processes, but some don't. In the case of estates or elderly sellers the pitfalls may be numerous. Various selling methods have been discussed in other chapters, but here are a few most commonly used:

1. Bank appointments
2. Advertisements

3. Dealers
4. Mail and local auctions
5. Selected collectors
6. Trades for usable commodities
7. Bid boards
8. Bourse tables at meetings

The collector who voluntarily places his coins on the market for a particular reason holds one point of view — the retail one. The dealer obviously clings to the wholesale price level, with perhaps some flexibility if the coins in question are of top quality. Other collectors expect to pay prices somewhere between those offered by the dealers and those asked by the seller. The whole process becomes a kind of sparring match, with the seller exploring the various market trends. The casual seller who is in no hurry to dispose of his coins certainly can do better than the collector who is meeting a deadline, yet there is no need to become panicky under any consideration. Quality of the coins involved will always be a prime consideration, a fact that should serve as a lesson to the careless accumulator of coins with limited potential. Frequently a collector who has completed all issues and series in a given grouping, feels a flush of accomplishment and decides to switch to another challenge. This type of seller is in an excellent bartering position because he has become well known through his achievements.

Bad health or occasional loss of interest may prompt a collector to sell a large collection. Such a person will need to feel around in the market for possible outlets. The experienced numismatist who has mostly accumulated coins all his life will find disposition of a large collection to be a grand adventure into a new level of tactics and price quotations. Through correspondence and personal contacts the seller will be able to establish an approximate median or middle ground from which to dicker.

Financial difficulties, usually not resulting from coin collecting, have forced the disposition of valuable collections on very short notice. Under such a condition the seller may not be able to use advertisements, mail auctions and other time-consuming methods. Buyers are quick to sense the urgency of the situation and will bid as low as possible on material offered. However, it is always possible to sell quality coins at fair prices, where both dealers and other collectors are brought in on the bidding.

The occasional death of a prominent coin collector strongly stresses the need for an orderly inventory of all coins that may be left to non-collector beneficiaries. The subject is far from a pleasant one for discussion, but its possibilities are real and should be viewed in a realistic manner. We all hope to live to be at least a hundred but a few of us may not make it! Nothing beats a good set of records in a bank box.

Recently a methodical Texas collector passed on and left an outstanding inventory of all coins and currency. He had photographed the rare items and had meticulously recorded the various buying prices. His wife and a bank officer were able to dispose of the estate to advantage over an extended period.

Many of the large coin collections stored in bank boxes have been dumped in with limited cataloging and description. A small percentage of such collectors operate on the "sly", because wives may not approve of extensive buying of expensive coins. Such collectors postpone proper pricing as an ameliorating gesture in case the wife takes an unsuspecting look in the lock box. These tactics may lead to a serious problem at a later date. But in all fairness to wives, it should be explained that they generally are happy with their husbands' hobby. In fact, many of the large collectors who use safe deposit boxes for their coins are women with an advanced interest in numismatics.

Many urgent requests are received from heirs who have just found valuable coins around the house or in bank boxes. Most of these persons have exaggerated opinions on the worth of such windfalls, but occasionally a real choice hoard comes to light. "How much are they worth?" "Where can I sell them?" etc., are the questions asked most often. Many scan the yellow pages for a listing of coin dealers, others buy coin catalogs. The lucky person who finds coins of this kind usually wishes to sell them at his own prices, but a reasonable seller sometimes emerges from such a lot. This type of collection is the exception not the rule in numismatics, yet some of the greatest rarities have appeared in old leather pouches and trunks.

The market for coins is not unlike that for antiques or the various commodities. The seller is at a distinct disadvantage only when he has collected items at excessive prices or has favored the issues of limited potential. The harum-scarum collector who has acquired perhaps several hundred pounds of marginal and very low-premium coins should not expect to obtain full retail prices, except by some stroke of luck. Trading may be a good way to dispose of large quantities of rolls, bags and circulated sets, unless the seller desires a more liquid transaction.

The average John Doe in numismatics may contend he is not interested in special selling deals and gimmicks. He has an ordinary "vanilla" type collection for sale with a $5,000 value. Most of the coins involved should sell at a good profit, a few at a slight loss. He would like to sell all at once but he would break them down to suit. Everybody seems to want to buy the gold coins and popular sets, while the dull issues are not in such sharp demand. He can make all kinds of trades but they may be harder to sell than the coins he is offering. He doesn't want full retail prices but he would like to get more than the wholesale quotations. He is in no big hurry but he hasn't time to visit all of the possible outlets. His wife is looking over his shoulder and he wants to show her that coin collect-

ing is a profitable hobby. How can he sell such a collection to advantage in the next month or two?

The answer to the above collector's selling dilemma may lie with a good coin dealer who can use much or all the collection. Most of us tend to overlook the dealer as a friend in need, yet he may not always be in a position to buy quantities of coins that might move better through other channels. An advertisement in a good coin journal probably would move such live items as gold, commemoratives and choice sets to advantage, while direct sales to other collectors frequently bring top prices. Mail bids and auctions will always sell the live and choice items, but such an approach may leave a heavy residue of the slow-moving coins. Bank appointments for a hard "look-see" examination of the collection are effective to a point, but buyers generally prefer to select the items in strongest demand. Bid boards in the larger coin stores may be helpful in selling the better coins, but again the collector will be left holding much of the least desirable items. The bourse table at meetings is an excellent sales approach for the average collector who wants extensive contact. Tables at meetings of this kind are largely manned by regular dealers, but some of the smaller associations permit collectors to operate tables of their own. This is not an uncommon occurrence where a collector desires to liquidate his holdings by payment of a fee for use of the table as a non-dealer.

No effort is being made to give the appearance that selling a coin collection is a grand affair requiring extreme finesse and skill. But it is a known fact that many persons can get top prices for what they sell, while others do not have the knack for some reason. Time after time a collector has sold choice coins, only to have them sell again on the same floor at much higher prices during the same day. There is nothing fatal in this little quirk, and it merely happened that the original seller was not posted on the market. On the other hand, a seller may be asking too much for his coins because he is not aware of weakness in the issues involved.

Advanced collectors who offer for sale a large number of expensive coins may wish to move them through a dealer on a consignment basis. This can be a rather slow method but it offers a control on the sale. Even smaller collections may be sold as a unit in this way where no special urgency is involved. The consignment approach is especially effective for groups of coins like commemoratives, gold, foreign crowns, etc. Where a collection up for sale contains a number of slow-moving items, the seller usually likes the unit or consignment basis as a means of passing on such coins to advantage on the coattail of the desirable issues. "You have to take it all to get the gold and rarities," is the standard remark of the seller who realizes he has some deadwood in the inventory.

A dealer will frequently pay top prices for certain coins he needs for wealthy customers. Collectors are sometimes stunned by high prices received at coin stores, not realizing that the dealer will be able to pass on his purchase to a particular collector who has been searching for the items involved. Many fussy numismatists will pay almost any price for certain top-quality issues that stand out as brilliant, uncirculated gems. It is not unusual for the better commemorative half dollars to sell far above catalog if they are in flawless condition. Such coins deservedly command premiums over the average specimens.

However, the seller should remember that going prices, rather than catalog quotations, predominate in any transaction. Many of the live issues may be selling higher than the catalog listings, while the slower groups may be temporarily depressed for various reasons. Because of this fact the seller should acquaint himself with market trends. Possibly some issues have advanced since available catalogs were issued.

The young collector who wishes to sell a $1,000 collection for college expenses may follow many of the routes described for the larger collectors. The success of his disposal effort will depend much on the length of time he has held the coins and the nature of the inventory. A little shopping around will tell the seller much about the course he will need to pursue. It may lead through dealers, other collectors or an advertisement. Of course, all collectors cannot possibly have for sale only the gilt-edge, live material, an important fact for the sellers to remember when they start accumulating coins again. It has been aptly said that to know how to buy coins, the collector must first sell some. All of the mistakes he has made show glaringly when he places them on the market.

## CHAPTER TWENTY-FOUR

# By Way of Observation

*Five Indian Head Cents, Obverse*

Coin collectors are as different in their tastes as other people, yet we frequently wonder how the real numismatist and the casual accumulator ever got so crossed up. The eager collector keeps asking how he can use the hobby as a miniature stock market for profit, while our old conservative friends won't let us off the hook to waver and recommend coins for future enhancement. Many of our advisers insist we generally lean too strongly toward the speculative influence that has been rampant in coin collecting for several years. But a trend is a trend for all of that, and the news must follow the trends. A few of our simon-pure friends call to suggest that no coin writer should even hint that the hobby is one devoted to making money.

But we must face the facts. About half of all United States collectors are hard buyers and sellers. Meaning, of course, that the numismatic aspect must step aside when necessary to make way for the investor, speculator and dabbler who seems here to stay. The complete coin sets and rare items bought to be held in permanent collections are still popular, but we must also make way for the glamor issues — gold silver dollars and proof sets — that have entered both collector and speculative ranks.

All coin writers get caught between the right and the left of the collecting group, a fact that causes us to recommend that all hobby-ists who collect, dabble, speculate or invest, just go on about your happy business. Some people raise tomatoes and flowers as a hobby, others raise them to sell. Disposing of the surplus may not be bad in either case. Trading and trafficking in coins is the principal delight to many good collectors.

Reports from the large World centers tell of an enlarged run for gold coins of every kind. It is estimated that the citizens of France have hidden away in hoards more than three billion dollars worth of gold in all forms. Each spiral in the bullion market has seen the French, from peasant to tycoon, rush to the bourses where "Napo-leons" and other gold coins are available. Gold bars also are a favorite hoarding medium.

In any country permitting the legal acquisition of gold as coins or a commodity, it has been largely purchased for speculation or plain hoarding against inflation. There is no way to estimate the amount of gold coins and bullion held secretly in Switzerland, but it must be tremendous. Deposed dictators, kings and big speculators have reportedly stashed away gold in all forms in this country. with some emphasis on rarity in the case of several numismatists. Swiss banks have been heavy holders of gold for a long time and it has been finding its way to other countries since 1955.

Gold coins in the United States make up a fairly constant inven-tory, although they now may be imported into this country without license if made prior to 1960. Previous to this recent liberalization there was a kind of churning around of such coins as were placed on the market locally from time to time. Prices of $10 and $20 pieces have increased around 250 per cent in the last two years, largely as the result of higher gold bullion prices. Official U.S. price now is $42.22 per ounce but the "free" price recently touched $130 per ounce in World Markets. Gold demand has increased most in the Middle East.

The gold hysteria has made many new coin collectors in the United States, just as the recent silver run attracted an extended following in that direction after 1964. The yellow metal is no longer used for coins in most countries, a fact that has made all gold coins numismatic items of a sort. Though not rare, there simply are not enough gold coins to go around among the new collectors who would like to get their feet wet in the exclusive club. This expansion has spiraled the prices of coins offered to the neophytes, who have become excited a bit late in the mad scramble for a few gold pieces.

Recent reports from Iraq, Iran, Saudi Arabia, India, etc., tell of large gold shipments to those countries. In most of the Middle East regions the sheiks and wealthy hoarders don't mind paying up to 10 percent more for gold coins than the prevailing prices in Switzerland. Small buyers will take gold on a surplus or spin-off basis at even higher prices. Gold hoarding in these areas dates back to perhaps 500 B.C.

Opinions differ sharply over whether gold prices will continue upward. Coins will move at prices considerably higher than their bullion value, but some form of stabilization is certain unless an official jump is recorded in the bullion market. Higher gold prices from a monetary standpoint would mean an actual devaluation of all currencies tied to the yellow metal. The United States has fought any formal devaluation of the dollar through higher gold prices, and the future remains a big question mark.

The Indian Head cent refuses to take a back seat to any other United States issue. This friendly little coin was minted from 1859 through 1909 and has become a kind of American institution. Though neither rare nor expensive in the common dates, a few of these coins may be found in nearly every household that is inclined to keep trinkets and momentos around. Most youngsters under 18 years of age have never seen one, simply because parents have kept them tucked away as if they were great rarities of the future.

However, the sudden appearance of a dozen Indian Head cents in an estate usually prompts a few urgent-telephone calls from the finder to a coin store or an experienced collector. "These Indian Heads are in good condition. How much are they worth?" the young caller asks rather frantically. The chances are 20 to one the precious coppers are dated between 1880 and 1909, are badly worn and are worth perhaps 20 cents each.

But we should not be too pessimistic about this little matter. Occasionally a caller will announce he has just found a handful of old Indian Heads, and among them are a dozen or so that are dated in the 1860s and 1870s. Whereupon the "callee" promptly warns the caller to hold everything until he can get to his house. He would like to see the copper cents right away, he urges with a posed calmness, because he needs these very dates for his collection! No wonder our party being called is so excited. Nice Indian Head cents dated between 1865 and 1878 sell for $15 to $200, although those worn slick will not bring such prices. You can bet that the party getting such a call will drop whatever he is doing and rush to the caller's house with the hope he will find a nice 1877 date in the lot. But there also is the possibility the caller has tried to sell the coins to every coin store in town and there is no chance to buy them at any reasonable price.

And while giving our secrets away on values, perhaps it would be smart, fair and informative to place reasonable prices on the common, badly worn Indian Head cents dated between 1890 and 1909— the kind usually found around the house. The rather "slick" cent of these later dates is worth about 20 cents; one a little better, around 30 cents; one with the word "Liberty" showing plainly on the headband, about 60 cents; and one with a minimum of wear, perhaps $2.50. The choice, uncirculated Indian Head cent is rarely found by chance, but when it turns up it will bring close to $15 in the common dates.

To the hundreds of owners who have run on to little hoards of Indian Head cents and made frantic calls for help on appraisals, the answer usually will center around the small word "Liberty" on the headband of the Indian girl. If this important marker is worn off, the coin has no special value in the common dates. Mutilated, burned or rusted coins are worth little more than face value and are avoided by all experienced collectors.

The Indian Head cent has long been popular with collectors because it is relatively easy to complete the set. Many dates are scarce and rather expensive, while most dates are cheap in worn condition. The highest priced coin is the 1877, yet it barely falls in the rare class. One very large bank reported it did not receive more than a dozen Indian Head cents in an entire year in deposits from customers. Upward of two billion were minted in the 51 years of ssue, but most of those that did not wear out seemed to have found their way into almost everybody's trinket box.

A surprisingly large number of professional people in large cities are avid coin collectors, according to a recent survey. Doctors, attorneys, bankers, merchants and industrialists are prominent among the prosperous group who have drifted into numismatics as their major hobby. The biggest one of all may be your next door neighbor.

Reasons for becoming collectors are numerous among the influential element that quietly goes about the accumulation of both the better items and the commoner, bulky material. An oil operator inherited a dozen old coins from his grandfather; a doctor read that gold coins were sure to advance some day; a banker gradually obtained valuable coins from customers who wished to dispose of them or merely turned them in; a utility executive started collecting coins as a boy, and a merchant found a box of old coins in his deceased father's effects.

Then we have the more dashing type of collector who literally caught fire when he read press reports of activities in proof sets, gold, rare coins, silver in general and silver dollars in particular. A good nudge from a coin dealer or a collector friend probably sent the eager novice on a buying spree that hasn't stopped yet. New enthusiasm is hard to beat in the field of numismatics.

Large gold coins have been particularly popular with the professional crowd for 20 years. This issue afforded a kind of investment item that seemed nearer foolproof than the more speculative coins of high collector value or low face value. However, many of the wealthy collectors preferred rarities and choice type coins, and in accumulating them became expert numismatists in their own right. Roughly half of the professional group acquires coins to hold as collectors, while the other half buys and sells on an investment, speculative or short-term basis. The whole hobby has become so mixed up that we have 10 million persons playing with coins for a dozen good reasons.

Occasionally a tremendous collection will come to light through death or an unusual circumstance. All the while our next door neighbor had been acquiring choice coins as a numismatist and enjoying them all by himself. However, such a loner is strictly an exception to the general rule. We may have many quiet collectors, but not that quiet.

Probably the most notable example of big-time coin collecting on a quiet basis was that of an Indianapolis industrialist who put to-together nearly all of the United States rarities, plus many from other parts of the world. And at a cost of only 51/2 million dollars! This grand assembly job was done so quietly that very few people knew about it. The wealthy collector was a real plunger and price was no object.

Most of the novices — rich or poor — need guidance badly when starting as coin collectors. They may be able to buy large amounts of coins as mature business men, yet they may also be inclined to accumulate a vast collection having no special sense of balance or direction. In simpler words, the adult who comes into the hobby experiences the same pitfalls as the young boy scout who starts collecting coins at the age of eleven. The only real difference is that the influential beginner makes a bigger splash.

The effect of the big buyer's action on both market prices and coin trends may be pronounced where rumors and press reports tend to influence his preference for such items as gold, silver, proof sets and rarities. His buying may be heavy enough to attract a false following that helps to push certain issues upward for a short time. And in some cases his judgement may be sound and fully justified. Many large market maneuvers in neglected coin issues are based on the premise that such issues have been selling too low. Good examples of coins in this category at one time were the 1950-D nickel and the 1955-D quarter, both of which staged spectacular rallies to new and sustained levels.

Collectors who start as adults tend to concentrate on fewer issues than novices in the younger ages. This fact mostly stems from the desire of adults to pursue some objective with a bigger push than the juniors can muster. They also have more money to spend as a rule, and are susceptible to investment and speculative transactions.

The spectacular appearance of old U.S. coins in present-day circu-

167

lation occurs just often enough to keep a few million searchers on edge. Ever hopeful that a real rarity will turn up in the next batch obtained at the bank, the patient scanner keeps looking for the end of the rainbow. But many of the recent discoveries came about in a more casual manner than could have been imagined even by the dedicated "stripper."

A U.S. three-cent nickel coin, dated 1881, recently appeared mysteriously in the cash drawer of the Stonington, Connecticut, post office. The very scarce obsolete piece had in some way been mistaken for a dime, but the postal employee didn't mind the error in the least. Coined from 1865 through 1889, the three-cent piece in cupro-nickel frequently was mistaken for a dime during the period of its issuance. Many of our senior citizens can remember when the coin circulated as an ordinary denomination that was held in mild contempt by the nearsighted. The one appearing at the Stonington post office was nearly uncirculated and worth perhaps $7. In this particular case it is possible that a Connecticut citizen found the coin in an old drawer or trinket box and carelessly passed it on as a dime — the old, old error.

The famous 1804 U.S. silver dollar has been represented for 60 years by speculators and sensationalists as a coin practically anybody can own with a little luck and patience. Tricks of all kinds have been used by advertisers who insist that the public should be on the lookout for these rare and elusive dollars. Currently such ads are running in various publications, but usually the big pitch at the end of the ads consists of an effort to sell the readers a coin book for perhaps $1 that could help the purchaser find many circulating rarities. Usually the 1804 dollar is pictured, along with a list of fabulous buying prices of a dozen or so rare coins believed to be outstanding. The catalog sales effort is strong. And sometimes it works. It is all legitimate, but the chance of finding an 1804 silver dollar in circulation is perhaps one in a billion.

Millions of words have been written on the 1804 silver dollar, both as a phony and a genuine coin. The thought of finding such a dollar still remains so intriguing that many innocent people are looking for one in a casual sort of way when they happen on to a few silver dollars of any kind in an old drawer or trinket box. But the serious and experienced numismatist hardly gives it a thought.

The charm of the Kennedy half dollar does not seem to let go, and especially those dated 1964. Well over a billion have been coined, of which 433 millions were dated 1964 and were of 90 percent silver content. It looks as if the clad issue, dated after 1964, will finally help to break the logjam. Certainly the Kennedy half dollar now free from silver, should do the trick by flooding every cash register in the country. Surely the hoarders will catch on and permit such a cheap "model" to circulate freely. By every rule of numismatics a nickel and copper half dollar should be ignored as a collectors' item. The 1964 half dollar will remain closely held because of its high silver content and original collector appeal. Even so, the issue of 433 millions of that date will guarantee that the coin will never become a rarity.

People all over the world regarded the 1964 half dollar as a kind of commemorative coin, and not as the regular issue it really was. In such countries as Spain, Italy, West Germany and various Latin American republics, the original Kennedy half dollar was eagerly sought as a medal or memento. Tourists reported it was an excellent tipping medium, but the chief trouble was that they could not get the coins before leaving this country. The natives of other countries are already smart, in that they chiefly want the 90 percent silver, 1964 issue. The later 40 percent silver halves are acceptable but not eagerly sought, and especially so in West Germany.

To the millions of people who have Kennedy half dollars hoarded as a kind of investment, it looks now as if silver bullion prices will be the controlling factor in their enhancement. With such a large number of the 1964s outstanding, they never can be rare but they will remain as notable mementos. The 433 millions that were issued would scatter out over a large area under any sort of demand. The coin simply is not a rarity.

For some reason the Roosevelt dime, first issued in 1946, was not extensively hoarded. All dates are readily available in circulated condition, but a few are scarce as uncirculated coins. This situation contrasted sharply with the entry of the Kennedy half dollar in

1964, possibly because coin collectors and hoarders were not so numerous in the mid 1940s.

Nearly all collectors continue to dream of discovering a large hoard of valuable coins in some far-away or unsuspected place, and under conditions permitting their acquisition at attractive prices. Possibly an old lady in the 1880s and 1890s had a penchant for throwing aside dimes and quarters. Now her grandson has decided to sell the several thousand coins. He has no idea of their value but they must be worth something above face value. And, oh yes, he has several gold pieces he would also sell. There are four or five $3 gold coins in the scarce dates. The owner had never seen one before, but they will go along with the lot if sold promptly. He would like to get his money out of the coins for another purpose.

The foregoing situation sounds like a nice dream, yet it has happened many times. The active collector who keeps his irons hot may not run on to such a juicy lot, but he will find many smaller collections in his travels. It is better to offer a fair price for choice collections owned by estates, non-collectors, etc., than to attempt to buy them at a small fraction of their real worth. However, many experienced buyers will first ask the seller to name his own price. In this way they feel justified in paying only the amount asked — even if it is rather low.

The constant pursuit of coins needed in a collection is a great joy to the serious collector. He may take home rolls of coins from the bank and give them a good going over, or he may search in unsuspected places. But he is always trying to fill in that blank space that annoys him.

The investor and speculator are looking for "sleepers" that are still thought to be available in rolls and bags. He buys and sells coins as a commodity, not as heirlooms. He makes all of the coin shows and keeps his ear to the ground. Yet he makes his part of the mistakes while buying hard and selling hard. This man is a new addition to the numismatic fraternity, and one who has managed to make the more common coins into a marketable product. He has his place, but the veteran collector tends to frown on his activities.

And so some people collect coins for fun; others for profit.

# CHAPTER TWENTY-FIVE

# Numismatics Today

*The Philadelphia Mint as it appeared shortly before the Civil War.*

Several sensational developments in numismatics occurred since the first part of 1969, with both gold and silver in the limelight in a greatly liberalized form. The Treasury Department all but let the bars down toward free movement and disposition of both silver and gold coins, a bold step that is expected to start a sizable flow of foreign-held coins toward this country. The long-range effect on prices of coins as both bulk material and numismatic items is difficult to predict, since collectors and speculators in this country must absorb the imported surplus from such countries as Switzerland, France and Canada. Apparently they will be able to do it without difficulty, since gold is held in such high esteem in regions where the monetary standards are a bit shaky. General World demand will be a prime factor in the market for silver coins as bullion.

Recent recommendations or rulings of the Treasury Department follow:

1. Congress has authorized minting of both silver and non-silver dollars bearing the likeness of David Dwight Eisenhower. The half dollar now carries no silver.

2. All silver has been taken out of U.S. coinage of regular issue.

3. The 2.9 million scarce silver dollars now held in Treasury vaults are being sold to the public on a combination fixed-price, bid-sale basis. Most are uncirculated "cc" dollars.

4. The export ban has been lifted on all U.S. silver coins.
5. Private melting of silver coins of the U.S. is permitted.
6. The importation, without license, of gold coins made before 1960 is permitted. Continued importation of very rare gold coins, minted after 1959 and having special numismatic value, will be permitted without license. Common gold coins minted now may not be imported.

All of the six provisions or recommendations were sought by coin collectors but it was hardly expected that such a sweeping liberalization would be forthcoming over a short period. No action was taken toward lifting the ban on free movement or ownership of gold bars, except those recognized as having definite numismatic value.

Elimination of all silver in the Kennedy half dollar surely should cause it to circulate freely, something that has not happened up to this time. Competition with a new Eisenhower silverless dollar could also have a reverse effect on the half dollar's continued reception as a hoarding medium. The new dollar certainly has been an exciting addition to U.S. coinage, even in a debased metal.

The Lincoln cent may be the commonest U.S. coin, but it continues to be the favorite among young collectors who are able to ease into the hobby via the least expensive route. On and on the novice searches for premium Lincolns in circulation, while slowly graduating to more advanced collecting that calls for purchase from dealers of the key coins necessary to complete this interesting series. The tenderfoot is satisfied with the usual circulated specimens at first, but he soon wants the much more expensive uncirculated coins as his appetite sharpens and his badly worn originals begin to look a bit shoddy. The first switch to Lincoln cents for beginners dates back to about 1945.

Increased interest in Indian Head cents continues to be reported from all sections of the country. This fascinating little coin has been discussed several times, but it is a kind of mainstay with many new collectors and hoarders who remain on the fringes of numismatics. Correct grading is of extreme importance when acquiring the Indian Head cent, since the value of a badly worn date, such as the 1877, may be less than 10 per cent of that of an uncirculated specimen. Indian Head cents did not go completely out of circulation until around 1930. They turned up regularly at banks in large deposits, but tellers started holding them out as something special after 1933. These obsolete copper cents make excellent gifts for young collectors who may need a little push toward a more advanced course in numismatics.

Several financial publications have been giving increasing space to coin collecting as an investment possibility. Emphasis usually is placed on the long-term aspect of the hobby by these special writers, who obtain most of their information through interviews and not experience. The various syndicated columnists, along with such publications as the Wall Street Journal, have greatly increased the mail and telephone calls of the coin writers who are expected to keep up with developments in numismatics.

A great swell of interest seems to be developing in coin collecting, following a vast plateau period that saw expensive rarities reach new heights. The hobby has become both a field for the real numismatists and a dabbling ground for investors, speculators and hoarders who are willing to wager a big pile of coins against a good size bankroll that the future will see scarce coins scarcer and the precious metal ones in gradually improved demand. Each collector and hoarder has his special reasons for his actions, with the whole accumulative action being regarded as an exciting game. The year 1973 seems to have been one that gave stable wings to the flight of coin collecting toward a greatly expanded hobby. The old coins, like real estate, will not be more plentiful in the future.

In my line of work as a coin columnist I am constantly receiving letters and calls from both serious collectors and the curious accumulators who look on coins as a means toward some projected end. An analysis shows that inquiries are divided roughly half and half between numismatists and speculators of a sort. Of course, curiosity over a few old coins around the house finally comes to a head in many cases. Some of the questions most commonly asked follow:

1. Are silver certificates still valuable and worth holding?

2. Should I continue to accumulate and hold 90 per cent silver coins?

3. Will gold coins keep going up, or will they pay their way from and interest standpoint? What effect will liberalization of gold importation laws have?

4. Should I buy rolls for the long pull? And what kind look best?

5. I have a loss in proof sets. What should I do with them?

6. I got caught with a big inventory of low-price circulated Lincoln cents and various dimes. Should I hold them or put my money in something else?

7. What medals should I buy, if any? Does a complete series of this kind have merit?

8. Is the Kennedy half dollar of 1964 worth hoarding; as silver or as a coin?

9. Are the various foreign proof sets genuine collectors' items?

10. Will commemoratives boom again? Why do they go out of style?

11. What circulated coins should I look for to hold for the future?

12. What type coins appear most promising?

13. Will silver dollars increase enough in value to warrant holding them?

14. Are complete sets of recent series a good investment for the long pull?

My wife is frequently my severest critic, but she is always fair. She casually asked me, "Now that you have been asked all of these questions, what are you going to do with them? What have you been telling all of these people?"

At best a man can have his own thoughts relating to the future. The title of this chapter is NUMISMATICS TODAY, and not to-morrow; and therein I have an "out" against trying to answer any of the above questions. However, just let it go on record that I am commenting on them as I see them. If I had all of the answers I probably wouldn't be noising them around. I'll leave guaranteed answers to the ultrasmart crowd that gets paid for their services as "forecasters." But I'll make a good try anyway.

And so we see from the questions asked that numismatics today involves a hectic cross-section of thinking among all types of collect-ors. The whole hobby is in a kind of status quo position, with parti-cipants asking one another questions about the future. We have seen the effects of overpromotion in the early 1960s, the neglect prior to 1950 of the worthwhile type coins, hoarding of questionable material during the recent boom, and a gradual departure from basic numismatics in favor of accumulative plans. And now for answering a few of the questions previously listed.

The common circulated silver certificates simply should have been turned in at the proper time. Many were held out for numismatic reasons but at the present they have no special value. The uncirculated ones in bundles of 100 may eventually be in demand, but at the moment they command only a small premium. Final redemption figures indicate that a comparatively large number of common silver certificates were held back.

The 90 percent silver coins are tied closely to the price of silver bullion, since they are not scarce in their own right. If the price of silver should remain under $2.00 per ounce, holders of silver coins will be lucky to get an annual enhancement of six per cent on their investment. A much higher silver price would carry the price of silver coins upward, since the melting ban no longer prevails.

Gold coins will be affected by gold bullion prices, but not to any exact extent. The small denominations already are selling at many times their bullion value. Since the heavy gold coins are not really scarce or rare, they will move up and down in an approximate relationship to bullion prices. Denominations up to and including the $5 piece have almost suddenly taken on a new value as trinkets, collectors' items and jewelry, rather than a form of bullion. The heavier pieces have increased in demand largely from a weight and hoarding standpoint. Liberalization of import laws should increase our supply of gold coins, but the World attitude toward gold as a monetary unit will ultimately determine the desirability of gold coins as a hoarding medium.

Coin rolls, if properly selected, should prove just as attractive as single coins. If the coins in a roll are desirable as singles, then the roll itself has numismatic appeal. Recent circulated rolls hold little favor where the single coins carry no real premium. However, a number of such rolls may be "sleepers" for the future, and our dislike for them now may be wholly unjustified. Collecting coins in rolls becomes a matter of taste, conviction and speculation, with most of us wishing we had put aside a few rolls of 1950-D nickels, 1949-P half dollars and a dozen other scarce issues that were readily available. To be perfectly frank, however, it is doubtful whether anyone will get rich from most of the clad coinage of 1965-72, even in rolls. For some reason ordinary coin rolls are repulsive to the veteran, puritanical collector who deems any items so plentiful as having no numismatic value. Rolls put aside between 1935 and 1956 prove that the practice was not such a bad one after all!

Proof sets originally were struck for fussy collectors who prized them for their beauty. Now they are being struck for the masses who have somehow caught fire from the publicity going along with their issuance. The former trading and occasional selling of proof sets has given way to speculation and a desire to hoard. Some 36 million sets have been struck since 1955, an important fact for future consideration. The similarity of one set to another tends toward a sameness that may also affect the demand for these sets in lots of hundreds and thousands. The jump in issuing price from $2.10 to $5.00 per set may have at least a temporary effect on the value of sets issued after 1956, but not necessarily so. The conclusion is that the millions of people who have a dozen or so of various proof sets have nothing to worry about. They own the numismatic items they want, as such. To the thousands who own proof sets by the hundreds and thousands, they simply will have to ride out the market as they would in any other commodity. General economic conditions will be a prime factor in the future market for the some 36 million proof sets now around.

During the big coin boom of the early 1960s a large number of beginners acquired recent circulated and uncirculated coins of little or no numismatic value. They now find themselves holding these rather glamorless coins at a considerable loss. It is entirely conceivable that another coin boom will come along and take them out at a profit, but the main question revolves around the cost of holding such inventories at sacrifice of interest return on capital. The moral to such a story is not difficult to see. Where speculation is the motivating influence, it is best to dabble in prime coins that always have a market.

A kind of medal hysteria seems to be sweeping the country. Those offered range from magnificent specimens sponsored by governments and recognized societies to a large number of questionable items that are little more than trinkets, mementos and souvenirs.

A well struck, well-meant medal carries with it a noble thought and a depth of purpose. A cheap medal that is struck for profit alone is not much better than a political badge or keepsake. The collector should be selective in his purchase of medals. The striking of only a limited number does not always dignify a medal, but it may increase its value.

The 1964 Kennedy half dollar caught the fancy of the whole world and it was hoarded from the day of issue. Just as the coin had begun to circulate a bit in 1967 the silver bullion boom came along to keep it in the selective class. Since 433,460,000 were minted and they are mostly put away, this coin should always be very much like the Columbian Exposition half dollar — something a *little* special but nothing to get excited about. From a statistical standpoint the 1964 Kennedy half dollar is largely a bullion factor. But from a curiosity and rumor standpoint it is a coin worth holding.

The various foreign proof sets now being issued are priced considerably higher than our own in some cases, with quantities minted being much less to make scarcity a possible factor in the future. Some collectors object to private distribution of these sets in a way that gives the middlemen a greater profit than the issuing governments. However, such sets in the past have held their values very well as numismatic items. Where foreign proof sets are distributed within reason, both from price and mintage standpoints, they may be considered numismatic items. However, there is always the danger of pricing themselves out of the market when in competition with U.S. proof sets.

Commemorative coins stand high as true numismatic material. A complete U.S. set is a highly desirable addition to any collection. These coins seem to be selling at improved prices, and they should be in better demand. A type set is adequate to cover the field, since overproduction in the mid 1930s did much to shut off their popularity. These coins undoubtedly will be leaders in the next coin boom, both those in silver and gold.

Many requests are received from collectors who regularly look through large quantities of change in an effort to find scarce coins. They all want to know what to hold out among the many marginal coins that barely make the grade. One accumulator already mentioned stated that he often held a coin in first one hand, then the other, all the while wondering whether it was worth keeping. One good rule is to hold out only those circulated coins that show a genuine premium, grade for grade, in reliable pricing mediums. Unless, of course, certain common dates are needed for a special purpose. One collector wrote that he first listed the scarce circulated coins he wanted, then generally hewed to the line in his search.

One type coin is as important as another in a set, but some are much scarcer than others. In the very early series, collecting becomes largely a matter of upgrading and not mere acquisition in many cases. Type collecting probably represents the most sensible approach to basic numismatics. Type coins generally have remained in strong demand long after the bulk material has fallen out of favor.

The silver dollar clamor has grown from a face-value venture of 1960 to a strong premium demand for these oversize coins. They are not scarce but they have finally got into fairly strong hands that are willing to promote them as something rather special. Eventually the silver dollar should ebb and flow with bullion requirements, since the common ones are so readily available in singles and rolls. This coin is not an easy one to figure from an investment standpoint, because it now is both bullion and a collector's item of a sort. General economic conditions will affect the value of the silver dollar in the future, just as it will affect quotations on proof sets and low-premium coins in general.

Complete uncirculated sets of recent issues look attractive for future demand. It is still possible to obtain such sets in the various series starting after 1930, although many dates and mint marks are becoming scarce. For those who are looking 10 and 20 years ahead, complete sets of any kind may prove profitable.

I see the forecasters and crystal ball operators are getting back into the picture again. Some of them all but give the subscriber a guarantee of a big future profit. The chief difference between them and me is that they charge for their tips; I don't. Seriously now, I have tried to discuss the hobby as I see it, with no strings or guarantees attached. But one thing I am sure of. Coin collecting will continue in a big way.

Pattern coins and trial pieces were commonly struck at the Philadelphia mint prior to 1900 in an effort to develop and select the most acceptable designs for general issues. Some of these patterns were almost identical with the types finally agreed on, yet a few were rather ornate and sophisticated. The engravers were apparently given a general or specific idea from which to work, then attempted to come up with acceptable designs within the limits of the assignments. Plainness usually triumphed over the fancier types when final decisions were made.

Patterns have depicted Miss Liberty in a dozen positions, ranging from only a head and neck to a full sitting or standing lady of great elegance. The rejected pattern dollar of 1872 and the half dollar of 1859 showed Liberty in a full sitting position and attired in gorgeous robes. The toying around of the engravers produced many interesting designs on the obverse (heads side).

Among the most unusual patterns were the ring (holed) gold dollars of 1852 and the 1884 five-cent piece with a large octagonal hole in the center. But they didn't make the grade as regular issues. All through our coinage history, beginning officially with 1792, numerous patterns and trial pieces appeared for examination. Many of the rejected specimens were admittedly more beautiful than the designs finally selected, because an air of practicality seemed to prevail in mint circles.

Our mint experimented with Washington and Lincoln nickels in 1866, $4 gold pieces in 1879 and 1880, and an international gold coin valued at $10 in 1874. The last was intended to be negotiable all over the world at a standard face value, but it did not materialize. Patterns were technically experimental pieces struck ahead of types finally accepted. They got into the hands of collectors and are available occasionally at auctions or public sales. But they are very expensive. In many cases a single pattern coin was struck in various metals, including aluminum, nickel, copper, silver and gold.

The $4 gold pieces struck in 1879 and 1880 were perhaps the most beautiful patterns ever issued. The stunning head of Miss Liberty is shown with both flowing and coiled hair, and the general appearance of these pieces is outstanding. These coins also were struck in aluminum, copper and a special white metal. The 1879 patterns were reportedly given to members of Congress, since more than 400 were issued in gold.

Thus the $4 trial piece in gold was doubtless our most extensive excursion into the pattern field, a fact that makes the 1879 flowing-hair type currently available to collectors in proof condition at about $12,000. The 1880 pieces are several times higher and are considered in the ultra-select class. This experimental piece represented an effort of the mint to strike a gold coin of the approximate value of the gold coins of several other nations. In numismatic circles the $4 gold piece is known as a "Stella," since it has a star on the reverse and carries the wording, "One Stella—400 Cents."

The annual proof set dilemma has been getting close attention from the Treasury Department, with emphasis on elimination of duplicate orders, a sharp reduction in the number of sets allowed per order, and use of special equipment or checking aids to discourage promiscuous ordering of sets by mere friends or special agents of purchasers who wish to resell them at a profit. Much of the ordering procedure of late has been a kind of legal subterfuge that has been difficult to detect by mint officials.

The 1968 and 1969 sets were limited to a maximum of 20 per order, but still many dealers and speculators also ordered the full limit of sets in the names of relatives and friends. The net result was the same as if one person has been allowed to order 100 to 200 sets, since the dummy purchasers involved simply passed on the unwanted sets to the schemer who did the original planning. However, in many cases it was possible for the mint to trace and consolidate duplicate orders where one address was used, a fact that helped to throw out deliberate attempts to order more than a fair share of sets. The limit now is five sets per order.

Prior to 1964 there was virtually no limit on the number of proof sets that could be ordered. The mint simply accepted the orders if they were within reason and filled them as they could. Total demand was such that the mint could handle large orders along with the small ones. The 1964 orders for the first Kennedy sets completely flooded the issuing mint in a few weeks and it was evident from then on that a limit on each order would be a necessity. Even after reviewing and reapportioning the 1964 orders it was impossible to meet the demand. The Kennedy image caused many to order proof sets for the first time.

Even the 20-set limit for 1968 and 1969 was not small enough to prevent a shortage of sets among those ordering a little late. Orders were shut off in less than a week in November, 1968, for the authorized 1969 sets, leaving thousands of genuine but slightly tardy collectors without an opportunity to obtain sets through original channels. Also, thousands of sets in early 1969 found their way into the hands of speculators who had either ordered them in some manner or purchased them legitimately.

Present plans for 1974 call for a limit of five sets per order, with a close check for duplicate orders. Such a small number might enable all collectors to obtain proof sets directly from the mint, as they were able to do for many years after 1950.

Doubtless a more effective enforcement provision could be established if the limit were spelled out as so many "per person," and not a certain number "per order." The word "order" seems to legalize attempts at chicanery to an extent that the Treasury Department can do little more than shame the speculators who send in several orders under various names. The proof set has become a kind of American institution, since a large number of neophytes want these sets as something special at a low cost. However, the acquisition of proof sets has made coin collectors of thousands of beginners.

California gold pieces represent one of the most interesting coinage periods of our early struggle to meet the need for small change. These small coins were struck in denominations of 25 cents, 50 cents and $1.00 by private firms that found the method an excellent way to convert some of their bullion into negotiable money. The tremendous boom around San Francisco required many more coins than were available, and certainly small gold coins of certified weight and fineness were much more acceptable than gold dust or various promises to pay. These miniature gold pieces were struck from 1852 until about 1882, their demise having been brought about by a law preventing private coinage.

California fortune seekers soon learned to recognize the genuine gold coins, but doubtless many were struck from gold of questionable fineness. The acceptable pieces always spelled out the value or denomination of the coins in one form or another, with "Doll," "Dol," "Dollar" or "Cents" having been a requirement. The later imitations appeared with "California Gold" on them, but they did not show a denomination. It is possible that many of the coins without declared denominations were struck from full specification gold, but they did not find ready acceptance prior to 1880.

The small California gold pieces were struck in both round and octagonal shapes, a mixture that caused no confusion in general acceptance. For many years after 1882 these coins passed among collectors at or near face value, but they now command very high premiums. The imitations and copies came on the market later in various grades. The first ones probably were of real gold (about 14 karat), while the debasement finally ran on through the gold-filled, gold-plated and gold-washed categories. The imitations now being made are little more than trinkets or cheap souvenirs. Serious coin collectors would do well to include a few pieces of the genuine California gold pieces in their inventory, although they will find them rather expensive.

Visitors in Washington, D.C. should be sure to include the Smithsonian Institution's famous coin collection in their rounds of the city. A recent addition was the fabulous gold coin collection of the late Josiah K. Lilly, a 6,000-item assembly valued at more than $6 million and acquired through a special act of Congress via through the tax credit route. Mr. Lilly secretly acquired the vast collection over a comparatively short time, with cost a secondary consideration where rarity was involved.

After the death of Lilly in 1966 the giant collection came to light. He had been purchasing coins on a secret basis in an effort to approach or achieve completeness of issues of the U.S. and other countries. Included are a number of so-called "unique" coins, of which only one of its kind is known or available.

The Smithsonian probably has the world's greatest coin collection. It is housed in its National Museum of History and Technology section. Many of the coins displayed are obviously so rare that they may be seen only at this place. New collections are being added.

Coin collecting trends in late 1973 have undergone a rather gradual switch. A national dilemma, fad or even a rumor can twist the habits of collectors who largely neglect to evaluate various reports that may have little substance. Economic and monetary developments also have been distinct factors in the rising demand for certain groups that are now near the head of the list in preference. Of course, metallic content, special redemption provisions and new issues can also influence trends for a time. Novices are much more susceptible to gossip and promotional schemes than seasoned collectors who tend to stay with their earlier choices.

It requires more than casual research to determine what coins or issues are most popular among collectors generally. Some variance in tastes will be found between regions, but composite favorites for the country as a group are possible to determine if enough questions are asked and representative sales outlets are surveyed.

In preferences listed below, only the premium issues that must be purchased are considered. The more common coins found in and held out of circulation are not necessarily included in the tabulation. A special effort has been made to contact coin stores and bid boards in completing a limited survey of current trends.

The first 10 groups listed are in order of highest popularity. The remaining groups are not listed in strict order of preference, but approximately so where representative sales activity justifies a rating. Regional acceptance can affect the rating popularity of a few groups where ethnic and geographical influences are evident.

Uncirculated type coins
Silver dollars
Gold coins
Proof sets
Commemoratives of U.S.
Franklin and W.L. half dollars
Currency
Miscellaneous uncirculated U.S.
Barber dimes, quarters, half dollars
Foreign, all kinds
Large U.S. cents
Ancient and medieval coins

Roosevelt and Mercury dimes
Jefferson and Buffalo nickels
Lincoln cents, scarce to rare
Indian Head cents
Washington and S.L. quarters
Medals and tokens
90 per cent silver coins
Obsolete U.S. coins
Kennedy half dollars

The above list is based principally on the better cash buyers and not the accumulators who largely look for premium coins still in circulation. The latter class is seeking such small-premium coins as Lincoln cents, Mercury dimes and all 90 per cent silver items. In mail transactions alone such issues as medals and Lincoln cents probably would score higher than shown. In the field of trading and minor speculation among new collectors, the Lincoln cent would rate near the top in any list.

Recently a young collector wrote excitedly about U.S. obsolete coinage and asked for a guideline that would include this interesting category. The chief confusion in the young man's mind centered around the difference between a truly obsolete coin and the various other old coins that represent nothing more than early types of denominations still being minted.

Actually experienced numismatists differ among themselves over what makes a coin obsolete, as compared with the finer points that brand them early issues that now have little resemblance to their forerunners. The large copper cent of 1793 certainly does not resemble the Lincoln cent of today, yet technically it is nothing more than the first type of our one-cent piece. The truly obsolete coin usually is one that has been discontinued officially from either a denominational or a radically changed metallic standpoint. Our half dime in silver (1794-1873) was technically a five-cent piece and actually carried the lettering "5 C." for a while, yet it hardly would be considered merely an early type of our present five-cent piece in cupronickel. The half cent in copper (1793-1857) is obviously an obsolete coin on every count.

Many ordinary coins that were simply discontinued are regarded in some quarters as obsolete, but they are not technically in this classification. Among such issues would be the gold coins, silver dollars and 90 per cent silver coins in general, all of which just petered out from one cause or another. It is true they are in a kind of maverick class, yet resumption of their minting is not beyond the realm of possibility. The silver dollar has been coined only in spurts and hitches since 1794, although it looks rather dead right now as an ordinary circulating medium. Gold coins were removed as legal tender in 1933, and their position in the obsolete field is largely a matter of interpretation.

True U.S. obsolete coins by general agreement follow:
Half cents in copper (1793-1857).
Two cents in copper (1864-1873).
Three cents in silver (1851-1873).
Three cents in nickel (1865-1889).
Half dimes in silver (1794-1873).
Twenty cents in silver (1875-1878).
Trade dollars in silver (1873-1885).
Three dollars in gold (1854-1889).

Some of the earliest types of the various denominations were so radically different from the present-day types of the same denomination that many collectors prefer to regard the older issues as obsolete. This controversial separation applies to such issues as the first silver dollars, large copper cents and the original gold pieces showing no denomination. Thus obsolescence, in a liberal sense, applies to such coins as may be singled out by the collector. Age alone or simple change in type should not be confused with the true obsolescence that goes along with official discontinuance of a denomination.

The trade dollar never was meant for general circulation, but it is a true obsolete coin from a numismatic standpoint. It also is an outstanding offbeat piece that carries an interesting history, with the use of silver to meet World competition having been back of its conception and use.

United States collectors of coins in the upper price brackets have become increasingly wary of certain foreign rarities that have been offered for sale as genuine issues. Many of the counterfeits are believed to have been acquired through dealers who were fooled by the natural appearance of the coins, the bold approach of the swindlers and the high prices asked for the phony specimens. The manufacturing process apparently has centered around the necessity for making the forgeries appear old and colored to the right degree.

The New York Times News Service recently reported from London that superb copies of antique gold and silver coins have upset the market for the genuine items in this category in both England and the United States. The report further states that collectors who paid up to $2,100 for one piece now wonder whether the newly acquired rarity was forged last year in a Chelsea apartment from old, melted-down watch cases. The counterfeits were so superbly made that they deceived many dealers. The purchasers seemed entirely satisfied until experts at the British Museum determined with strong microscopes that the coins were forgeries. Both the metals used and the general appearance of the illegal coins were deceptive enough to deceive the rather advanced numismatist.

The fact that the reproductions were offered at rather stiff prices greatly reduced suspicion. Some were offered at auction at special "reserve" prices, a scheme that tended to prevent the bogus coins from selling by making them appear as very choice rarities.

The London dispatch of the Times reports that the defendant, A.M. Dennington, was extremely skilled in casting the reproductions from molds manufactured from powder employed by dental technicians in the making of ordinary dentures. Dennington counterfeited more than 40 rare coins of different reigns dating back to about 1075. After a long court trial he was found guilty and sentenced to two years' imprisonment on the six charges that he fraudulently influenced collectors to purchase forged coins by giving the impression they were buying genuine old coins. Dennington had claimed that he made the coins only as replicas, and not for sale as genuine antiques.

There is no way to determine whether a considerable number of these spurious coins were marketed in the United States. The greatest danger in acquiring doubtful coins lies in the purchaser's inability to lay the counterfeit alongside a genuine coin for comparison. Where an authenticated specimen is available, the collector may know in advance by checks and balances whether the coin under study is the real McCoy. It is believed that many museum pieces are counterfeits. In a famous old Russian collection it was difficult to separate the forgeries from the genuine coins, even in a single issue. A cast copy of a fairly recent coin is rather easy to detect, but the very old coins were so imperfect that they may be almost perfectly copied by the casting method. Doubtless the various replicas on the market today have hurt the standing of many genuine old coins that certainly deserve a better fate.

Collectors who are interested in resumption of commemorative half dollar coinage should write representatives in Congress, expressing their reasons for the numismatic need of such special pieces. Numerous small movements favoring additional commemorative coins are cropping up here and there, but no concerted and co-ordinated push toward this end has been noted. Occasionally an occasion or accomplishment grand enough to warrant a special coin comes along, yet a special medal or Congressional action usually suffices. At the moment medals of one kind or another seem to be filling the gap, but numismatists generally feel that these mementos, both official and unofficial, hardly carry the prestige that a commemorative half dollar would have.

The first coin of this kind was the Chicago Columbian Exposition half dollar of 1892, honoring the 400th anniversary of Columbus' discovery of America. The last was the Washington-Carver half dollar of 1954, paying tribute to Booker T. Washington and George Washington Carver. During the 62-year span of issue 48 different types of commemorative halves were coined to honor important people, places and events. Principal reasons for discontinuance of these special coins were the lack of demand and the doubtful importance of some of the events commemorated.

Congress also was besieged with petitions to strike commemorative half dollars honoring so many occasions that the coinage finally died of its own weight. However, the collecting public now would purchase such half dollars by the millions if they were issued. Again, the final selection of two or three types for actual coinage would doubtless involve almost endless wrangling among the supporters of the large number offered as nationally suitable. But this should not prevent issuance of coins honoring many of our outstanding events and achievements.

An analysis of proof set coinage throws a great deal of light on the potential of proposed commemorative half dollars. In 1950 only 51,386 proof sets were sold, yet in 1964 3,950,762 sets were issued and several times as many could have been distributed. The collecting public now is ready to grab at about anything issued of a special nature. Actual selection of a limited number of commemorative half dollars would be the big job.

A 1964 English penny that had no right to get into circulation has become a great rarity that escaped the melting pot through an error. The story connected with this interesting coin doubtless will encourage U.S. collectors to continue their search for valuable coins still believed to be in general circulation. The owner of this unique penny, an Ohio dealer, states that in 1954 a small number of English pennies bearing that date were struck in London to test the dies. Since no order for the pennies materialized, all of the trial pieces, except the only known surviving example, were destroyed along with the dies. It is interesting to note that this lone specimen was retrieved from circulation and has been valued at about $25,000. Pattern coins, or trial pieces, frequently are struck by all mints ahead of the design or type that ultimately is approved.

The elusiveness of many U.S. coins continues to baffle collectors who feel the various specimens of certain large issues should eventually show up from some source. Up to this time many coins that should be common are so scarce that only museums and the wealthiest collectors own them. The anomaly applies to coins struck in both gold and silver.

Particularly rare are certain issues of $20 gold pieces that should be around in quantities, but they aren't to be found. Since 1933 collectors have wondered about the possibility that such double eagles as the following will appear from an unknown source or hoard. Did they remain in government vaults for lack of public demand, or were they almost entirely turned in during the famous "Roosevelt" redemption call of 1933-34? How could so many have been minted and virtually disappeared among certain dates? A few of the currently rare double eagles that were minted in large quantities follow:

| Date | No. Minted | Unc. Price |
|------|------------|------------|
| 1921-P | 528,500 | $ 7,500.00 |
| 1926-D | 481,000 | 1,500.00 |
| 1927-D | 180,000 | 60,000.00 |
| 1927-S | 3,107,000 | 3,250.00 |
| 1929-P | 1,779,750 | 4,000.00 |
| 1932-P | 1,101,750 | 5,500.00 |

Any price placed on the value of the 1927-D $20 gold piece would be rank guesswork. It is believed that a nice specimen would bring $60,000 at auction. In 1947 the 1924-S $20 gold piece sold at auction for $2,500. However, a few years later a hoard of these coins was found in Europe and the price fell quickly to about $300. The decline struck many other double eagles when the initial flood of Swiss-held U.S. gold struck this country in the late 1950s. But such dates as the 1921-P and 1927-D have not been uncovered in any appreciable numbers. Their possible appearance remains a threat but apparently a remote one. Indications are that certain dates of double eagles minted after 1920 did not circulate as heavily as those issued during the 1850-1920 period, although those coined at Philadelphia in 1922-23-24-25-26-27-28 did manage to circulate extensively all over the world. Just why the "S" and "D" mint double eagles of the same period turned out so scarce is a guess.

The 1909-S $20 gold piece, with a mintage of 2,774,925, brings about $200, while the 1913-S double eagle with a coinage of only 34,000 may be bought for around $500. Many of the comparatively small issues of certain years prior to 1890 now sell for less than $225. Although 445,500 double eagles were minted in 1933, none supposedly got into circulation and it is illegal to own one for some nebulous reason. Others may be legally held.

The 1929-P $5 gold piece is perhaps the greatest enigma of all of our rare gold coins. Even with a mintage of 662,000 only a few have appeared as collectors' items. Many numismatists believe that larger numbers of this elusive coin will be found, while others contend that only a few left government vaults before the ban on gold coins during Roosevelt's first administration. An uncirculated specimen sells for about $2,250.

Reactivation of the old San Francisco mint in 1968 has resulted in mixed emotion among coin collectors and banks that have been unable to get the "S" mint coins in the usual process. Now known as the San Francisco Assay Office, the old plant is for all practical purposes exactly what it was before its discontinuance in 1955—a branch mint. The shutdown at the time did not appear a very wise move.

Re-commissioned in early 1968 to strike proof sets with the "S" mint mark, the old mint was also pressed into broader service with the coining of 1968-S cents and nickels, plus foreign coins on a fee basis. The scramble of collectors to acquire a few of these coins brought on the usual clandestine channeling to dealers and favored customers principally of West Coast banks. A great deal of effort was required to force a more reasonable distribution of the 1968-S cents and nickels. The same maneuvering took place in 1969 and for a time the "S" coins of this year were very hard to get at face value.

Actually the speculators have done such a good job of cornering the post-1968 "S" cents and nickels that they still remain as something a little special if purchased by the roll or bag. High interest rates on money has helped to jar loose many large hoards.

In the beginning mint officials thought they could force free distribution of 1968-S cents and nickels if they minted enough to remove the scarce tag. Plans also called for mixing these new "S" coins in bags with worn and circulated coins from other mints, a kind of trick that would place the new "S" coins in a form of automatic circulation. Even this sly plan was only half effective, since bank tellers and the usual grapevine soon spotted the mixture. Dealers were able to obtain the mixed bags of coins and sort out those bearing the "S" mint mark, for sale to collectors at a premium.

It seems a long way off, but various patriotic and numismatic societies are already planning and pushing for issuance of suitable coins and medals to commemorate the 200th anniversary of the signing of the Declaration of Independence. A great deal of sparring will take place between now and 1976, but it is entirely possible that both an official government medal and commemorative coin will be authorized for public distribution. Such a medal was struck in 1876 and offered for sale that year at the United States Centennial Exposition in Philadelphia. Annual Centennial Medals already have been authorized for release on each July 4 until 1976.

Doubtless a large number of privately struck medals also will be issued to commemorate the 200th anniversary of American Independence. Several medal societies and clubs have been organized to furnish members with a certain number of medals over a long period. They use such subject matter as may seem appropriate, but in most cases the private medals are planned in advance along some topical theme. The year 1776 probably will tempt most of the medallion clubs to make their best showing in honor of a great past event. It seems a long way off now, but time goes pretty fast.

Several large coin hoards have come to light recently as a reminder that collectors a hundred years ago were stashing away certain issues that appealed to them for various reasons. Many of these accumulations were held out in the remote past when the coins were worth little more than face value. As they appear again from old hiding places they may be worth from 50 to 200 times face value as desirable rarities. Denomination and condition frequently are the determining factors in prices received.

However, there is quite a difference between the true old hoard and the vast collection that may have been put aside since 1940 by a smart speculator who "just happens" onto a large number of coins he has held for profitable disposal. The word "hoard" somehow brings out the petty larceny in both seller and buyer, and actually little hocus-pocus may be justified in transactions resulting from a great "discovery" that may border on the commonplace. In the strict sense of the word, a hoard is a hoard, but the connotation may easily be overdrawn by some promoters who simply have an antique complex. There is something exciting about acquiring old coins that supposedly came from a mysterious hoard — maybe from the coffers of a sunken ship or a crock in somebody's back yard.

About 1896 a giant hoard of early U.S. large cents and half cents was discovered, supposedly having been buried about 1830 in old crockery jars or kegs. This very large and authentic accumulation consisted in part of brilliant uncirculated 1828 half cents and 1818 large cents, coins so beautifully preserved that they appeared to have been minted the day before discovery. For many years it was possible to purchase coins from this hoard at rather low prices, but finally upon full absorption by collectors the 1828 half cent and 1818 large cent gradually edged higher to a more realistic level of $125 and $150, respectively. It is known that in early days our mint stored and shipped copper coins in wooden kegs, and it would have been possible to obtain a whole kegful at face value.

Small hoards still are a prime source of rare old coins. Recently more than 1,700 old half dollars came to light from an unsuspected source. All were dated prior to 1837 and their current collector value ranged up to $100 each for the better dates.

The most exciting coin hoards of recent years have come from sunken ships that went down in hurricanes as far back as 400 years. Such shipwrecks were fairly common along the Florida and Texas coasts, and they are now yielding coins and artifacts of great historical importance. Most of the gold coins recovered have been in splendid condition but the silver coins have largely been damaged by exposure to the salt water. Where it is possible to certify that a rare old coin came from such a sunken treasure, it will sell for a much higher figure than a comparable coin with a more limited pedigree. Old records show that perhaps as many as 50 Spanish galleons perished in coastal storms prior to 1800, of which many went down along the Texas coast. Not all were carrying gold and silver coins in quantities but many were known to have been transporting both coins and bullion to Spain from Latin American colonies. State and national laws relating to such buried treasures are somewhat vague.